Beginning With Genesis

Beginning With Genesis

A Journey from Knowledge to Wisdom

William J. Wright

Foreword by Dru Dodson

RESOURCE *Publications* · Eugene, Oregon

BEGINNING WITH GENESIS
A Journey from Knowledge to Wisdom

Resource Publications
An Imprint of Wipf and Stock Publishers
199 W. 8th Ave., Suite 3
Eugene, OR 97401

www.wipfandstock.com

PAPERBACK ISBN: 978-1-6667-4319-7
HARDCOVER ISBN: 978-1-6667-4320-3
EBOOK ISBN: 978-1-6667-4321-0

MAY 6, 2022 9:28 AM

Contents

Foreword

A FRESH READING OF GENESIS is rare and welcome! Not only is Dr. Bill Wright's reading of Genesis fresh, it is deep and thoughtful, the result of years of reflection and study. Bill is an amateur in the best, classic sense—he interprets Scripture out of his love for it. It's not his job. He is a medical doctor, not an academic doctor of theology or Biblical exegesis. Yet his love for Scripture and the truth of God has made him one of the best students of the Bible I've ever run across. His favorite book of the Bible is not Genesis, but . . . wait for it . . . Leviticus. You know, the book that usually causes people to give up their read-through-the-Bible New Year's resolution.

In *Beginning with Genesis,* Bill's close attention to the text as he observes cycles and patterns pays rich dividends in understanding the author's intent. Too many exegetes try to psychoanalyze a biblical author, or they simply bring to the text their own intent and then use it for their own purposes. A mark of Bill's expertise is his conviction that the author's intent is embedded in the structure and the literary strategy of the text itself. This unwavering attention to the text, not being in a sense distracted by the events it is narrating, is a hallmark of an accomplished reader and teacher of the Bible.

Further, he takes Jesus' statement in John 5 seriously—that the text of Genesis testifies to the Messiah and our need for Him. Genesis has huge implications for evolutionary science and modern anthropology, with deep insights into the psychology and sociology of humankind. But for Bill, the first order of business before unpacking those implications, was to pay the price of due diligence in a deep, lively reading of the text itself. That he is laser focused on trying to better understand the author's—and the

Author's—message is abundantly clear, and laser focused on what Jesus said—that this remarkable text called Genesis testifies about Himself.

I recently retired from the staff of a church I helped plant twenty-eight years ago, Lake Valley Community Church in Hot Springs, Arkansas. As you may guess, there were many trials and tribulations as the church grew, and many joys and satisfactions. One of the joys has been to know Bill and his remarkable family. To sit with Bill before a whiteboard and discuss and debate the meaning of the Scriptures was a privilege. His thoughts challenged and enriched my own reading and teaching of the Bible, and I believe it will do the same for you.

Dru A. Dodson DMin
February 2022
Hot Springs, Arkansas

Introduction

ON A DISTANT MIDDLE EASTERN HILLSIDE, under a sky filled with stars and hope, an old and discouraged man believed God's promise to him of a son, and faith was born. Nothing has been the same since.

This book intends to join that man's journey: to see what he saw, to think his thoughts, to believe what he believed. And, as only those who have been blessed with an ancient history can, to lay that man—Abraham—to his rest and continue our journey with his son, and sons of sons, to see with their eyes and believe what God would promise them.

We begin with the opinion that Genesis and the Pentateuch comprise a tightly woven account of events that is much more complicated than meets the eye on a casual read. The stories can be understood on multiple levels and are interwoven to provide deep insights to those willing to allow their efforts, hearts, and imaginations to join the journey of faith.

I have been assisted immeasurably by writers and speakers who have undertaken their journeys to understand faith as demonstrated in these five books. I have brought into view the thoughts of Jewish sages like Rashi (1040–1105) and Nachmanides (aka Ramban 1195–1270), discussions found in the Midrash, and thoughts by recent and present authors as well as my own as to what the Torah is saying. I will try to draw the reader into the stories, to inspire asking, "How would I have responded there?" or "What must she have been thinking when that happened?" Any such habits learned from the stories of Genesis will pay great dividends when applied to the rest of the Bible.

Because the Bible is silent on certain things that go on behind the scenes but may be cautiously inferred, some speculation is used in this book to encourage the reader to become part of the story. Faith, after all, is an active process. I encourage the reader to have a copy of Genesis nearby, and to read along with an eye to the nuances that make insight possible and exciting. No one has a full understanding of Genesis, but as we explore together, new horizons will appear and call each reader to a better and clearer understanding of God's Word.

The title of this book is clearly a play on words: Genesis means "beginning." However, I mean it as two stages deeper than that. First, no matter how long this book becomes, or how many other tomes are stacked up with it, the reader will only be starting to understand Genesis—this is just a beginning. Second, I chose the title in the sense of Proverbs 9:10: "The fear of the lord is the beginning of wisdom, and the knowledge of the Holy One is understanding." Any search for wisdom and understanding, it seems to me, should begin with God's communication to us.[1]

The book is in sections. These sections are standalone, meaning they do not need to be read in order and can be skipped if the material is of no interest.

After an overview in Section 1, Section 2 puts forward my thesis that Genesis can be seen as a series of crises, which I number as cycles. Each cycle begins with a situation in which there is, absolutely or at least relatively, NO HOPE. BUT GOD intervenes in a LOVING WAY that BUILDS FAITH. The cycles are listed in table form in Appendix D.

Section 3 is an attempt to show in greater depth how what might seem like isolated stories are closely related by common (often unique) words and repetition of events, and their order of occurrence. These correlations are sometimes solely inside Genesis, but also relate Genesis stories to other parts of the Pentateuch. This section is designed to start the reader thinking more globally by piecing together the complex interactions found in the Pentateuch—with the tacit belief that there are seldom coincidences of similar order of events, places, or circumstances.

Section 4 deals with the construction of the Pentateuch. It demonstrates the complex, interwoven nature of the five books and is a partial rebuttal to higher criticism that leaves the impression that the Torah was patched together basically as a Jewish myth.

One of the techniques used in Genesis is the establishment of a pattern—the order of creation, say—that is repeated later, expanding the

---

1. Ps. 111:10: "The fear of the LORD is the beginning of wisdom; A good understanding have all those who do His commandments; His praise endures forever."

Prov. 1:7: "The fear of the LORD is the beginning of knowledge; Fools despise wisdom and instruction."

breadth of the pattern—the flood reverting (nearly) everything to the precreation state and proceeding in creation order to recreate the earth. I will use repeating charts with additional rows to keep tabs on these theme expansions.

As students of God's Word, we must always remember that Scripture has levels of meaning and differing depths by which we may understand it. The only verse God cannot use to speak to us is the one we are sure we fully comprehend.

Having spent years reading Genesis and listening to how other people read and understand it, I know that I will always be just *Beginning With Genesis*.

Section 1

An Overview

"You search the Scriptures because you think that in them you have eternal life; it is these that testify about Me."

JOHN 5:39

OF ALL THE WORLD'S histories, mission statements, documents, and truths throughout all of time, the most important is the first chapter of Genesis. Genesis 1 is God's statement "I created you. I created the earth and the universe and all they contain." From that statement flows all other Judeo-Christian theology, especially salvation, because in the absence of the Creator status, there is no moral basis for a need for salvation. "For God so loved the world that . . ." is a non-starter without the world created to love. "All have sinned and fallen short of *the glory of God*" is not compelling without establishing that *the glory of God* has a bearing on reality (emphasis mine). So, as a history, Genesis 1, though challenged by evolution and frequently made out to be another epic myth seen in many ancient cultures, is the seminal source; as a mission statement in the "who we are" sense, it has long been the model; and as a document, Genesis 1 is one of the most studied and written about of all time. As Truth, it is the basis for all other truths—including the rest of the Bible.

The infallible truth of Genesis is not only non-optional, it is imperative. Reading the Old Testament as unreliable ancient history and the New Testament as present truth entails a very real problem: the New Testament authors believed the Old Testament was present truth, and if they were wrong about that, they cannot be trusted on anything. Almost all the New

1

Testament books quote or reference Genesis, usually in the first few chapters.[1] To paraphrase C. S. Lewis' famous statement about Jesus and extend it to those writing about Him in the New Testament, either they are lunatics, or the devil of hell to be totally ignored, or they are telling God's truth. There is no in-between.

To those not questioning the integrity of the Pentateuch but unclear as to why to spend time reading, much less studying it, let me advise by revisiting a cliché from the 1990s: What Would Jesus Do? People sported buttons and bracelets with the letters WWJD as if asking the question solved the issue. Most of the time we cannot be sure exactly what Jesus would do. He routinely surprised the Pharisees—Bible scholars all. Some of his actions are still surprising today. He not only used a whip on the temple merchants, but it was also not a rash impulse—he made the whip himself.[2] Neither making a whip nor using it to clear the merchants out of the temple are actions usually anticipated by those wearing a WWJD bracelet.

But when he was facing Satan at the temptation, we know exactly what he did—he quoted Deuteronomy—three times.[3] It is always useful to know the answers while you are waiting for the questions. To that end, we need the deepest understanding of these Scriptures that we can get.

An additional insight into the importance of knowing the Old Testament stories comes from Jesus' use of parables. In Matthew 13 as Jesus is telling a string of eight parables, he is interrupted by the disciples asking, why the parables? His answer had to do with mysteries of the kingdom of heaven (v. 11), prophets not getting to see what the disciples were seeing (v. 17), and a quote from Isaiah pronouncing that the people's hearts were dull (v. 15). After the parables he quoted from Psalm 78 explaining that the parables utter things hidden since the foundation of the world. Here is the context: ". . . I will open my mouth in a parable . . . We will not conceal them from their children, but tell to the generation to come the praises of the LORD, and His strength and His wondrous works that He has done."

Jesus goes on to say that Jehovah "commanded our fathers that they should teach them to their children, that the generation to come might know, even the children yet to be born, that they may arise and tell them to their children." He explains the reason they should repeat the stories and

---

1. See Appendix A: The Bible without Genesis.

2. As did Gideon, Judg. 8:16; in future chapters we will note similarities between Abraham and Gideon as well.

3. Matt. 4:1–11.

instill them in their children's hearts: "that they should put their confidence in God and not forget the works of God, but keep his commandments, and not be like their fathers, a stubborn and rebellious generation, a generation that did not prepare its heart and whose spirit was not faithful to God" (Ps.78:2–8).

The disciples were slowly seeing with the eyes of faith that Jesus is the Son of God and the Seed of Abraham, but they did not understand the parables as he spoke them. However, after Pentecost they started seeing the Old Testament as Jesus' autobiography and were able to understand it and his parables. Perhaps Jesus was saying that the Old Testament stories prepare our hearts to understand the parables of the New (and Old) Testaments. By ignoring (or paying only scant attention to) the stories detailing God's power and faithfulness, we no longer put our confidence in God and therefore fail to understand his parables.

The richness of the Old Testament is enhanced by its structure (discussed in Section 4), by analogies (discussed individually), and by parallel stories allowing—even demanding—comparison. Examples are discussed, including one chart for simplicity. Here is an example of parallel stories, along with a quiz question:

1. I lived among the wicked at a time of God's impending judgment.

2. Two by two, we entered a designated safe haven.

3. God destroyed all men, women, children, animals, plants—everything.

4. Afterwards, I got drunk and was debased by my progeny. Who am I?[4]

Another important feature of Scripture is typology. This causes interpretive problems for some readers because of the constant question, how far can we go with typology? However, types are clearly part of biblical teaching and cannot be ignored. Consider, for example, Romans 5:14: "Nevertheless death reigned from Adam until Moses, even over those who had not sinned in the likeness of the offense of Adam, *who is a type of Him who was to come*" (emphasis mine). Also, Hebrews 11:19: "He considered that God is able to raise people even from the dead, from which he also *received him back as a type*" (emphasis mine).

In Section 4, I provide a summary of John Sailhamer's presentation of the carefully crafted structure of the Pentateuch. It is at the back of the book because many people have no interest in structure. But if you are one who

4. Noah or Lot (Lot and wife, two daughters, two angels). Did you get both?

appreciates an in-depth understanding of biblical design, I would recommend reading that section first. Very briefly, he sees a repeated basic unit of story, poetic segment, and epilogue. This is built into books, and books into larger units.

On examination of the story components in Genesis, two sub-structural elements can be added to Sailhamer's formulation to help elucidate the parallel structure: (1) each story starts with things getting worse and then (2) God intervenes. At least twenty-one times this happens encompassing the whole of Genesis (see Appendix D). In Genesis 1:2, "formless and void" plus darkness is remedied by the Spirit moving over the waters and God saying, "Let there be light."

In Genesis 3, Adam's disobedience, requiring just action, is followed by God cursing not Adam, but the ground. A pattern emerges: there was NO HOPE . . . BUT GOD. Further, it can be seen (often in the poetic seams that Sailhamer found to consistently produce unifying end times' statements) that ACTS or WORDS of LOVE follow God's redeeming action. This is followed by FAITH-BUILDING actions—frequently the establishment, clarification, or renewal of promises or covenants which are not random but occur as a result of a cycle of fostering events. Through consistency and repetition, the message of Genesis emerges: there is NO HOPE BUT GOD and through His ACTS of LOVE, our FAITH in Him increases.

Section 2

The Genesis Cycles

Earth, the Early Days

Genesis 1

"Now these things happened to them as an example,
and they were written for our instruction."

1 CORINTHIANS 10:11

BEFORE THE BEGINNING THERE was God. God had a story: a Lamb slain, a Book of Life, and names of saints written therein.[1] The phrase "before the foundation of the world" in Revelation modifies either "written in the book" or "the Lamb that was slain" depending on the translation—later and earlier translations, respectively. Either way, the creation is a series of quite purposeful preconceived events with the end of creating man and providing for his needs both with a perfect environment and a means of reconciliation with his Creator after an anticipated separation.

God started counting existence when he created the heavens and the earth "in the beginning." Also "from the beginning" God prepared the kingdom of heaven.[2] Thousands of years later Jesus proclaimed this kingdom "has come upon you,"[3] but its inception was from the foundation of the earth.

Nothing was random in the creation, and nothing is random in the inspired account recorded in Genesis.[4]

1. Rev. 13:8.
2. Matt. 25:34.
3. Matt. 12:28.
4. The importance of this non-randomness is why we included a big-picture glimpse

Cycle 1 starts with NO HOPE: "The earth was without form and void, and darkness was over the face of the deep."[5] Apart from the foreknowledge that a redemptive plan exists, this is a bleak beginning indeed. Formless, void, dark, cold, and water everywhere—an environment totally unsuited for human life. BUT GOD was hovering and said, "Let there be light." With that utterance the first redemption was on the books, and time started. God revealed Himself to the formless void that was the earth.

The first day had light and dark, a day and a night, but no time markers—no sun or moon. This is a source of criticism of the Bible as "non-scientific," but it is the criticism that ignores the science. A day is based on the earth rotating around its axis, not the sun "rising" and "setting." The lack of a sun to help humans keep up with the degree of rotation is immaterial—a day is one rotation. In the case of creation a sun was unnecessary as there was no human present to keep up with the first three days. Even now, people living underground for extended periods or through a polar winter have no trouble counting days based on the time each earth rotation takes.

The light was created by God, not by nuclear reactions in stars as is now the case. If the earth were spinning at its current rate, the length of day and night at any given spot on the earth would have been the same as it is now, but God was keeping the time: evening and morning, the first day. (Note we are not told what constituted evening or morning, just that they occurred.) In creation terms, darkness preceded the light even as now night is generally preparation for the following day. A bad night portends a bad day. Let me say that my commentary will be from a literal six-day creation viewpoint because I am looking for patterns in the Scripture that are repeated and therefore give additional meaning. God says there was evening and morning—a day—and that is the pattern I am looking for. I will let others debate what a creation day is.

The tendency is to read rapidly through the few verses describing creation. This is a mistake. Take a moment to think about what happened. In six days the whole universe as we know it—sun, stars, moon, sky, clouds, mountains, rivers, plants, animals, and us—was created from darkness, formlessness, and void. That is an immense project, so it should be a major surprise that all that was created on the first of only six days[6] consisted of

---

of how organized the Pentateuch is in Section 4.

5. Gen. 1:2.

6. Even non-literalists—most people, I would venture—should think proportionally; i.e., six periods and the one devoted to just light.

. . . light. It was not even the permanent lighting solution of the universe; the sun, moon, and stars were created on day four.

The day one light was the Shekinah glory of the Lord. It gets its own day to make a point. As discussed above, the kingdom of God was established from the foundation of the earth, and day one is the announcement. There is a kingdom of light and a kingdom of darkness, and God has separated them. You can choose your kingdom—in fact you must choose one or the other, for there is no middle ground. God made the separation. Further, He said only the light was good, which should help our selection but often does not.[7]

On the second day, the waters covering the earth were divided vertically above and below an air space called heaven.[8] Again, not much in the grand scheme of things: more than thirty percent of creation time gone and all we have are clouds and oceans that you can only see half the time. If you were somehow there, watching, you would still be treading water (there was nothing to build even a raft).

The typology, the revelation, is huge. Not only are there two competing kingdoms, but battles rage between them on two fronts: the earth physically and the heavens spiritually. Just as we must either be in the darkness or the light, we cannot escape these battles. Everything we do has physical as well as spiritual consequences. Everything to come is created inside the framework of days one and two.

On day three, the water below the heavens and the solid land below the water shifted to separate the water from dry land. This was an enormous geologic event. A continent, known to geologists as Pangaea, was formed with titanic forces unleashed: tsunamis, mountains uplifting, earthquakes, probably massive volcanic eruptions and lava flows. Whatever was here after Genesis 1:1 was totally changed on day three, and the process would be repeated to some degree during the flood in Genesis 7 and again in an event mentioned in Genesis 10:25: "the name of the one [son of Eber] *was* Peleg [whose name means divide], for in his days the earth was divided." This was the start of the shift of the tectonic plates. What reads like another casual day in pre-paradise in verses 9 and 10 was almost as big as the earth being created ex nihilo,[9] "out of nothing," in Genesis 1:1.

---

7. Gen. 1:4.

8. Gen. 1:8.

9. Rom. 4:17: "even God, who gives life to the dead and calls into being that which does not exist." John 1:3: "All things came into being through Him, and apart from Him

Here is one of the first lessons of the Bible: the two biggest geological events in the earth's history are recounted in three verses—Genesis 1:1, 8, and 9. The magnitude of these events goes largely unnoticed by casual readers of "Judeo-Christian fables" and children's Bible stories. Only those readers who pause to consider each verse, those who tell the stories over and over, who answer their children's questions and ask some themselves, start to experience the magnitude of those three understated verses. And so it is with the rest of the Bible—long, sometimes seemingly repetitive stories[10] about marginally interesting events and then one verse thrown in, the significance of which might be missed altogether were it not quoted and exegeted four times in the New Testament (in the case of Genesis 15:6).[11]

Picking up the creation pace a bit, day three included providing vegetation on the dry land rescued from the waters below. The vegetation not only completed the water cycle that keeps the planet rejuvenated, but the plants also came with seeds to reproduce after their kind.[12]

Why would a plant want to reproduce? In a non-creation model, seeds would have had to evolve. But why? In the big picture of creation, of course a Creator would want plants (and later animals) to reproduce, and "after its own kind"; but on an individual basis, why would a cabbage want to produce more cabbages? It would require a lot of work and energy expenditure, be of no benefit to mama cabbage, and the increased competition would be a detriment in times of nutrient or water shortages. How long would it take to perfect a seed? Did the original plants live that long?[13] Non-creation scenarios have a lot to answer.

After each day of creation, God pronounced the work-in-progress good, implying it had been bad— "formless and void" bad. (Just as the Tree

---

nothing came into being that has come into being." Heb. 11:3: "By faith we understand that the worlds were prepared by the word of God, so that what is seen was not made out of things which are visible." Rev. 4:11: "Worthy are You, our LORD and our God, to receive glory and honor and power; for You created all things, and because of Your will they existed, and were created."

10. They almost never are exactly repetitive. For instance, there are two listings of the Ten Commandments, in Ex 20 and Deut. 5, that are almost identical, but the difference is the basis of a major theological equivalence. This is discussed in Section four.

11. "Then [Abram] believed in the LORD, and He reckoned it to him as righteousness." Try reading this story ignoring what you already know about the significance of this verse, and notice how easy it would be to read right past it.

12. Gen. 1:12.

13. Even in an evolutionary model, presumably with plants reproducing by division, why would they divide and why would they develop seeds ever?

of *Life* in the next chapter implies *death*). It also raises the possibility that if it can change from formless to good, it can change back, as we see all the time when "improved" land reverts "back to nature" when not actively cared for.

The general process of creation, the pattern of development, seen in Genesis 1, is this:

Light (of kingdom)
Vertical separation (of water)
Horizontal separation (land/water)
Plants with their seeds
Signs (sun, moon, stars)
Birds/Fish
Mammals/Man

We will see this pattern again, most notably at the flood of Noah's time.

The creation week is completed in Genesis 2:13. God rested. This sets up another type, which is also repeated throughout the Pentateuch and carries with it New Testament and post-biblical implications and broad effects.

Verse 2:4 starts a section that requires much commentary because it appears to be a second account of creation.

Genesis 1 is not a description of what was created, but a description of the creation *process*. Famously there are two accounts of creation:[14] Genesis 1:1 to Genesis 2:3 and Genesis 2:4 through the rest of chapter 2. The first account is a series of separations:[15] light from dark, water above from water below, land from water, stationary from mobile, non-living from living, non-terrestrial from terrestrial, and finally not-in-God's image from man. Note that the light in verse 3, day one, denotes the presence of God on the earth, is a result of the establishment of the kingdom of God, and is different from the light in verse 15 (also said to separate the day from the night) which comes from lights in the expanse of heaven, day four. Plants (day three) sprouted before there was a sun providing light and timekeeping (day four). The "lights" in the expanse were designated for signs and seasons, which would later correspond with the festivals in Leviticus. That the sun, moon, and stars "give light on the earth" is mentioned twice: verses

14. This leaves out Gen. 1:1 as being its own creation story, as can be convincingly argued, for simplicity of discussion. The "and" starting Genesis 1:2 of course argues the other way.

15. After Leon Kass, *The Beginning of Wisdom*, 29–34.

15 and 17. As there was already light on the earth, separated from darkness (v. 4), these verses recount the changeover in the earth's light source on day four. Due to the enormous distances, God must have created the light path from each star to the earth; otherwise, the stars would not have been visible for centuries.

In the biblical economy, plants and animals are separated by two days of creation. In Hebrew the word for life is *chay* and for animal is *chayah*; in Greek the words are *anima* and *animalia*. The life is in the blood.[16] A further distinction in the creation process was between plants and animals on the one hand and man on the other. "Let the *earth* sprout vegetation . . . Let the *waters* teem . . . and let *birds* fly . . . let the *earth* bring forth living creatures" were the processes that created plants and animals, whereas "Let *us* make man in our own image . . . male and female He created them," and no "after their kind" distinguished the creation of man (emphasis mine). Blessings "to multiply" were given all around, but only man was told to subdue and rule over the earth.

The second creation account, starting in Genesis 2:4, is more focused. In Genesis 1, things are global; Genesis 2 is local and more personal. Genesis 1 has waters, but in Genesis 2 the water is moving in rivers, and the rivers have names. Names are given to animals and trees as well. Man is not just created as in Genesis 1, but God handcrafted man *(Adam)* from clay *(adamah)* and breathed the breath of life into him.

During the sixteenth century, Rabbi Judah Loew ben Bezalel (also known as "Maharal of Prague") wondered why man was the only one to be named after the ground—after all, weren't the animals created from the ground as well? His answer was that both man and the land or ground were created in a basic, pure status requiring cultivation to flourish and to reach their full potential; hence the afternoon walks with God in the garden. The animals were created "almost completed" with minds that do not have the same capacity for increasing in knowledge as the human mind.[17]

In an ACT OF LOVE God took care to plant a garden for Adam and provided a helpmate, Eve, so he would not be alone. The general commands God gave our first parents to fill, subdue, and rule in Genesis 1 are made specific in Genesis 2; in other words, instruction to keep the garden as well as restrictions against eating from the Tree of Knowledge of Good and Evil (TKGE), which added the ability to disobey and fail.

---

16. Lev. 17:10.

17. Hebrewversity.com, "Hebrew origins Adam's name connection ground", page 1.

We can get some sense of the topography of Eden and the garden from verse 10: one river that waters the garden divides into four. The garden must have been situated in mountains to allow water to divide into different rivers. Think of modern-day Tibet, where the snowmelt creates four major rivers and provides water for half of the world's population.

Word usages also highlight differences between the two accounts. In Genesis 1, God—*Elohim*—created the *eretz* (earth) of water, rock, sand and silt, but in Genesis 2:7 the Lord God—*Jehovah*—forms Adam from *adamah* (earth). Although never absolutely delineated, the Pentateuch maintains at least a soft differentiation between *eretz* and *adamah*. The instances of *adamah* are few as I will point out later.[18]

The presence of more than one creation story scandalizes Bible critics and squeezes apologetic harmonization attempts ("single story with two perspectives," etc.) out of believers. Two accounts must be contradictory, the thinking goes, and, in addition to the above variances, the stories do have different orders of creation. The same anxiety is *not* extended to the four Gospel accounts—not always identical and certainly with different orders of events. We see the overlap in Samuel, Chronicles, and Kings as well, with no corresponding felt need for explanation.

Let me make a case for chapter 2 as a "carve out" from the chapter 1 account: it happened at the same time and, with one exception, in the same order as the first account, and is separate because each telling sets up a pattern of events which will be repeated.

Genesis 2:5 finds our place in the big story: "no shrub of the field was yet in the earth, and no plant of the field had yet sprouted." That is day three at noon in the Genesis 1 account—after the dry land separated from the waters below the sky (v. 10), but before the vegetation appeared (v. 11).

God creates one man, Adam, for a special purpose. What Adam first sees is the day three noontime desert—no vegetation, no streams, no animal life: just a barren landscape. God then then continues with Genesis 1:11 creation by "let the earth sprout vegetation" including creating a beautiful and sacred place, the Garden of Eden, for Adam to live in and enjoy special communication with God. God gives the man instructions: "From

---

18. An interesting dichotomy in Gen. 1 is that all the animals, trees, etc., were created by *eretz* except man and . . . things that creep on *adamah*—Gen. 1:25 (the first use of *adamah*). In the next verse, it is everything that creeps on *eretz*.

any tree of the garden you may eat freely," and restrictions: "from the tree of the knowledge of good and evil you shall not eat."[19]

Creation proceeds as in chapter 1 with the making of lights, swarms of living creatures in the waters, birds in the air, and land animals. Eden was a sanctified place that God created for Himself where he could walk and talk with the chosen man at a specified time, the cool of the evening, so the man would know God and thereby INCREASE his FAITH. The man was given responsibilities such as naming the animals, and he was given a helper.

19. Gen. 2:17.

The Curses

Genesis 3

For our struggle is not against flesh and blood, but against the rulers,
against the powers, against the world forces of this darkness, against
the spiritual forces of wickedness in the heavenly places.

—Ephesians 6:12

Now these things happened to them as an example, and they were
written for our instruction.

—1 Corinthians 10:11

Whereas cycle one elicits discussion and controversy, **cycle 2** causes a
loss of focus because it is all too familiar—the garden, the snake, the fruit—
and too similar to Alice in Wonderland or Dorothy in Oz. The story is easy
to read along but not believe.

Allow a thought experiment to reset your focus as an aid to reading
these well-worn stories with fresh understanding. Imagine being presented
with a huge banquet table starting with salads and breads, then fruits, vegetables and casseroles, trays of meats, and particularly appealing deserts. To
help with the analogy, we have to say that you have never seen any of the
fruits, vegetables, or meats before—they have been gathered from remote
areas but are chosen for their good taste, not just because they are rare;
nothing is here such as, say, whale blubber which Eskimos eat in the absence of anything else. Think rambutan (fruit), rutabagas (vegetable), and

ostrich (meat), or some other suitable food that you have never eaten but could choose to please your tastes.

In the middle of the buffet sit two covered dishes, simply labeled Number One and Number Two. Your host points to a stack of plates and tells you to eat all you want, no charge, *but* covered dish Number Two is reserved for the host only and would be poisonous to you. He says to take your time, the food will be kept fresh and replenished, and he will check on you now and then. The host leaves. The tantalizing aroma of the food and the time of day have made you quite hungry. What would you do?

Do not read on! Stop reading and experiment with the above exercise. You are hungry and know nothing about any of the food around you. What would you do first? You need to get a plan before proceeding. Your plan will affect your understanding of the coming discussion.

Cycle two begins not where the first cycle left off as much as it heads to where the first cycle started—dire circumstances. Questions about the serpent/forbidden fruit story arise even before it is all out, prompting St. Augustine to comment that this is a story meant to be read by all and understood by few. The first question the story raises is, "Do you believe snakes talked?" That is, "Do you believe the story happened at all?" As discussed in chapter one and Appendix A,[1] Genesis 3 is not optional. Paul believed the story as told; he believed not just man's sinfulness and separation from God, but the talking serpent as well. He referred to the serpent in letters to the Corinthians and Timothy.[2] Was Jesus referencing Eden when he said we are to be wise as serpents[3] (which clearly Eve was not)?

Secondly, "How did a beast of the field know so much?" The serpent was familiar with knowledge of good and evil at the least. Scripture never says that the serpent was Satan or controlled by Satan, but implications are made. In fact, it is not clear that the serpent was a beast of the field at all, only that he was "*more crafty* than the beasts of the field that God had made"[4] (emphasis mine). In fact, we do not even know what the serpent looked like. The Hebrew word meaning snake or serpent is transliterated *nahas*[5] and comes from a root[6] differing only in vowelization and which is

1. The Bible Without Genesis.
2. 2 Cor. 11:3 and 1 Tim. 2:11–13.
3. Matt. 10:16.
4. Gen. 3:1.
5. *Strong's* H5175.
6. *Strong's* H5172.

also transliterated *nahas*. This root means to practice divination, to divine, observe signs, learn by experience, diligently observe, practice fortune-telling, take as an omen. There are three other Hebrew words for snake, but they are not commonly used. The prohibited aspects of the root word coupled with the nature of the Genesis 3 story seems to make serpent fit better than snake, but it is the same word for what Moses picked up to make his staff[7] and is clearly a snake in Proverbs 23:32 and 30:19. However, Genesis 3 is hundreds of years and a specific curse before the exodus, and things can change.

To give Eve some credit, we need to realize that she did not encounter a snake coiled up by the tree looking like it was about to strike. Imagine, as is conceivable, that this serpent was the *only* talking animal, and Eve was having a Balaam's donkey experience. (No one ever faults Balaam for listening to a talking donkey.) Also possible, and brought into perspective by the curse of, "On your belly you will go, and dust you will eat all the days of your life," is that the serpent had legs (certainly, or "on your belly" would not have been a curse) and wings (which makes the curse particularly pointed). A flying, talking serpent (a dragon?) could have been very per-suasive. In eastern cultures, particularly China today, dragons are seen as intelligent, friendly, and auspicious, portrayed with bright colors and four legs (without wings). They are celebrated and integral to celebrations; that is, the opposite of fierce, fire breathing, need-to-be-slain western dragons.

Alternately, in several podcasts and videos[8] Rabbi David Fohrman de-scribes another reason for the animal's credulity. Most animals are covered by fur, feathers, or thick hides; snakes not so much. Add walking like us and talking to us, and the this possibly was the one animal in the garden that was most like Eve and Adam.

In the story the serpent speaks of *Elohim* as in Genesis 1, not the more personal Jehovah as is used in the rest of the garden accounts. In dealing with the serpent, God put enmity between the seed (singular) of the wom-an and the serpent. Okay, to this day most women do not like most snakes. But verse fifteen states, "He [the seed] shall bruise you [the serpent] on the head and you shall bruise him on the heel." As Paul points out in the third chapter of Galatians, the singular pronouns and the historical facts point

---

7. Exod. 4:3.

8. See alephbeta.com, a site I highly recommend and the source of much information and stimulation of thought. It has a paid section but much is free; even so, the cost is well worth the price.

to this as foretelling Jesus' passion and death, which makes the serpent in the present story Satan, or at least his proxy. Also, Revelation refers to the "ancient serpent" as the "deceiver of the whole world."[9] In Genesis 3:22, God stated that "the man has become like *one of us, knowing good and evil*" (emphasis mine). "Us" refers to God as either an "imperial we" (Jewish interpretation)[10] or the Trinity (Christian view), but the scope of knowing is beyond created man—and, as the serpent also knew the difference, the implication is that the serpent was beyond the creation story.[11]

Why did a talking serpent have so much credibility with Eve? True he was crafty, but still, Eve was willing to trust the serpent over God or at least over what Adam had told her that God had told him. Further, the trust was not about the appeal of the food—she provided that herself—it was about life and death. Think back to the thought experiment. Would it have affected your actions if a smartly uniformed server came by checking the table and told you that the food in chafing dish Number Two was especially good and not poisonous as you might have heard? "Actually," he told you, "the host just wants it all for himself."

A fourth question is, "What did Adam and God talk about on their strolls through the garden?" Certainly, the topic was not TV or sports. The weather seems unlikely. Not politics. No vacation selfies or video clips. Perhaps God was teaching Adam about good and evil so that one day he could eat of the Tree of Knowledge of Good and Evil (TKGE) safely. Or so he would not want to.

A fifth question is, "Why had Adam and Eve not eaten from the Tree of Life?" It was next to the TKGE, both described as being in the middle of the garden.[12] Both trees had names, but the Tree of Life was not forbidden. It seems that a tree with those credentials would invite immediate attention. Again, to our experiment: how long would it have taken you to try covered dish Number One? Would the fact that it was separated from the rest of the food by being covered have slowed you down or drawn you to it? What about the fact that it was right next to the forbidden dish Number Two?

---

9. Rev. 12:9 and Rev. 20:2.

10. Like the Hebrew word *Elohim* being plural but treated as singular.

11. As part of his punishment, the legless snake would "eat dust" all of his days. Adam, made of dust, would return to dust, providing a tangential sense that the snake and Adam would do battle until the Seed arrived.

12. Gen. 2:9 and Gen. 3:3.

Perhaps, and this is speculation again, initially the Tree of Life had not bloomed; in other words, it had no fruit. The tree existed, but until there was sin there was no need for its fruit. Imagine Adam and Eve standing there—partially eaten fruit from the TKGE in hand, serpent smiling maliciously—and suddenly the Tree of Life right beside them blooms and puts out fruit as in time-lapse photography. The serpent, always quick with a phrase might have said, "Wow, I didn't see that coming." Eve would turn to Adam and say, "We had better hide." Adam, who hadn't said much all day, pointed toward the fig tree. That's how Jehovah found things.

Back to the text. God gave good and called it good. Eve decided other things were good for her. She *saw*, apparently as she thought God *saw* when He declared it good, that the tree was good for food (lust of the flesh), a delight to the eye (lust of the eye), and desirable to make one wise (pride of life),[13] so she ate. Obedience means *especially* when our senses tell us otherwise: "build an ark," "go to a land I will show you," "place Isaac on the altar" are commands that surely engendered at least a "what?" or a "why?"

John Milton in *Paradise Lost* faults Eve for not being on guard against deception. Why should she have been on guard? Because facing contradictory evidence brings up the issue of the greater good. Where is your trust: God, your senses, a talking snake? Eve went for two out of three—the snake confirmed by her senses. "Two out of three ain't bad" is usually the punchline of a joke—in this case a cruel one. "God alone" was the correct answer.

But Milton surely has a point. Eve was told in the deception that eating the fruit would open her eyes and she would know good and evil.[14] But, she already knew good—God had said that the creation was good; in fact, when man was included it was *very* good. She only stood to know evil by eating of the forbidden tree. Adding evil to a good life situation should have been seen as foolish.

Still, "lest you die" does seem like a poor deterrent to someone who had never seen death (at least not human death and probably not animal death, depending how long they had inhabited the garden). But, a Tree of Life implies death and raises the question of the extent of Adam and Eve's understanding. What did they know and when did they know it?

While we are on the subject of what they knew, another question springs up from when they ate. They didn't *see* they were naked; they *knew*

---

13. 1 John 2:16.

14. Gen. 3:5.

they were naked. Knowing is different from seeing: first, they were both naked and there was no one else in the garden, so why did it matter? Second, none of the animals had clothes; naked was standard. The nakedness they knew was more than fig leaves could fix. Hiding didn't help either, so when God said, "Where are you?" they gave up hiding as a misguided fix. What they "knew" was that disobedience had put a separation between themselves and God. They were outside his protection. They were bare. They may have still been standing in the garden and still been alive, but they were no longer "keepers" and were spiritually dead.

Adam, who should have been the deterrent for Eve, was not one. God had placed him in the garden to cultivate and "keep" it.[15] "Keep" means to guard, keep watch and ward, protect, save life."[16] Adam was not a ward to Eve or a guard to the garden.

In fact, when Adam did not stop Eve, he put himself in the position of knowing her death was certain and had to make a choice between fellowship with God *or* eating the fruit himself, breaking fellowship with God, and being with Eve. He could not do both. The First Adam was in the position that eventually the Second Adam would be in: stay with God or take on sin to re-establish a relationship with the sinful bride. Adam chose disobedience and hid from God. He quit walking with God. There was NO HOPE.

A seldom noticed aspect of this over-familiar story is the sounds we encounter. *Nahas,* the Hebrew word for serpent as mentioned earlier, is pronounced "naw-khawsh." The word is onomatopoeic in that it sounds like a snake's hiss. Adam and Eve hid, not because they saw God coming or knew He was due, but because they "*heard the sound* of the LORD God walking in the garden in the cool of the day"[17] (emphasis mine). They put more credence in God's sound than in His Word, or at least the sound made them aware of His presence, of which they were unaware when the snake was hissing.

Here we need a pause. Resist the impulse to race forward to the showdown in the garden, the punishments meted out, and their implications. Think for a minute about your actions in the thought experiment with the food. How did they compare with the actual events in Genesis? Admittedly the experiment would have been much more effective if you did not see it as

---

15. Gen. 2:15.

16. *Strong's* H8104, *shamar.*

17. Gen. 3:8. See Young's Literal Translation: "they hear the sound of Jehovah God walking up and down in the garden at the breeze of the day."

related to Eden (a situation not possible in a book on Genesis), but any time you spent getting into it has been rewarded proportionately.

Stop for a while and think through what we do not know. Why was there a TKGE in the first place? And Adam having failed to protect Eve, where was God? After all, no TKGE, no sin; or, if God had slapped the fruit out of Eve's hand and given her a good scolding, He would not have had to banish her from the garden, preserving his original plan.

Now that line of thinking should not ring true because it is not. The plan goes back before the garden, before the serpent, before Adam—indeed before the foundation of the earth. How does an invisible, all-powerful God demonstrate Himself to mortals? How to define love, grace, faith, and hope to a freewill-wielding group of created I-think-therefore-I-am-ers who will eventually decide there is no Creator?

The plan was to let unguided freewill go, to let it fail, to facilitate the failure so it could be seen as failure—one episode clear to all, the clock starts here—to avoid a vague "over time, man displeased God." The plan was—is—to demonstrate true love, and thereby God himself, for God is love,[18] by redeeming disobedient man from a situation that was his own doing, but from which he could not extricate himself. The plan is to allow sin to multiply in order that grace might abound.[19] The plan is to bring fallen human beings, one by one, to the kind of faith in God's power that God himself demonstrated when he called the universe into existence. The plan is for people to put their hope in the risen Messiah, their Redeemer, their source of new life in Christ, and be reconciled to God, having failed when left to their own devices, but now living in the power of Christ, walking with God again in a true understanding of sin, good and evil, and faith, hope, and love from God's perspective.

An objection to the plan as formulated is, "Could not God have created mortals to resist the corruption they faced in the garden?" Or, more pointedly, was God's grace "incapable of endowing us in the beginning with souls that were not inclined to rebellion," and how then "could His grace ever subsequently acquire such a capacity?"[20]

The plan addresses the heart of man. God wants to bring each heart to understand and be capable of unconditional love. He started by

18. 1 John 4:8 and 16.

19. Rom. 5:20 and 6:1.

20. Thomas L Pangle, *Political Philosophy and the God of Abraham*, 94.

demonstrating it himself,[21] then showing that even the ideal setting of Eden with only one distraction would not allow a human heart to get to unconditional love by itself. He then by his grace disciplines us[22] and trains us as sons and daughters to discern good from evil.[23] His grace aids those who are tempted.[24] The nature of unconditional love requires freewill, and freewill allows failure. God always deals with our hearts and was willing to give up Eden to bring us with Abraham to Mt. Moriah.

BUT GOD instead of cursing Adam, cursed *adamah*. The garden was changed, the earth was changed; thorns and thistles were added; the earth would only yield its fruit to hard labor. Adam, having failed as caretaker of the easy life, would have a hard one. He, and all mankind with him, would go from having one issue to complicate his day (do not eat from the TKGE) to having multiple complications and troubles to deal with.

Eve, for her part, had two additional punishments (all of Adam's problems fell on her as well—a thorn is a thorn, sweat is sweat): pain in childbirth and a "desire" for her husband.[25] This is the first of three uses of the word translated *desire* in the Old Testament. The second is in the following chapter regarding Eve's son Cain, when God tells him sin has a *desire* for him—a negative connotation. The third is in Song of Solomon, a love song, in a positive usage. Given the proximity of occurrences one and two, both in the narration and in consanguinity, it is safe to take a negative inference for Eve. Whereas the serpent and Adam received an explanatory "because" and Eve did not, some inference can follow that Adam and Eve's punishment is the same—that is, *toil*[26] for the produce from *adamah,* and *pain*[27] with childbirth are the same word (hence it is called "labor"). Since this curse and expulsion from Eden, the goal has been to enter back into

21. Heb. 1:3: "And He is the radiance of His glory and the exact representation of His nature, and upholds all things by the word of His power. When He had made purification of sins, He sat down at the right hand of the Majesty on high."

Matt. 25:34: "Then the King will say to those on His right, 'Come, you who are blessed of My Father, inherit the kingdom prepared for you from the foundation of the world.'"

22. Heb. 12:58.

23. Heb. 5:14.

24. Heb. 2:18.

25. Gen. 3:16.

26. Gen. 3:16: *Strong's* H6093: *itstabown.*

27. Gen. 3:17: *Strong's* H6093: *itstabown.*

God's rest, with disobedience always resulting in being barred from entering into that rest.[28]

In an ACT OF LOVE, Jehovah sacrificed animals' lives to make a covering for the sinners, a picture of the sacrifice and covering of blood on which our faith is based. The tunics he made were a picture of the tunics the Levitical priests would wear. The animals' deaths were a graphic picture for Adam and Eve of what death looked like. To guard the Tree of Life, God placed cherubim, again a type like the cherubim on the Ark of the Covenant guarding the Word of God as symbolized by the Ten Commandments.

GROWING IN FAITH as a result of failure is a hard thing to this day; obedience is a resistant lesson. Nevertheless, although Adam and Eve lost their place in the garden, it was still possible for Enoch, Noah, and Abram to "walk with God."[29]

Was Adam still alive when God took Enoch up?[30]

Cycle 3 starts with an embarrassing personal rejection and accelerates to fratricide. Here we look at Genesis 4, which begins with Eve conceiving and giving birth to Cain "with the Lord" (v. 1); the phrase "help of" was added by translators to assist the English. However, Eve's statement can also be taken as a prideful boast: "I have gotten a man-child *equally* with the Lord";[31] in other words, both produced a man. This attitude in mom may have been picked up by the son, as demonstrated by his actions later in the story. It is of further interest that Sarah, Rebekah, and Rachel all had trouble conceiving, which would have the effect of avoiding this tendency toward pride.

Adam named his first two sons for two things he received then lost in the garden: Cain means possession (of the garden) and Abel means breath; in other words, life (the meaning of "gotten" in verse 1— "I have given life").

What can be learned by examining why Cain was a gardener and Abel a shepherd? Several possibilities exist: (1) some people like working with soil and others like animals; (2) diversity helped put food on the table; (3) the boys did not get along; or (4) as suggested in the Midrash,[32] Adam separated them for a combination of reasons 1–3.

28. Ps. 95:11, Heb. 4:11.

29. Gen. 5:22, Gen. 6:9, Gen.18:16.

30. Yes, Gen. 5.

31. Gen. 4:1.

32. Meaning "to investigate" or "study." The Midrash is a collection of rabbinical

Multiple theories, guesses really, exist as to why God rejected Cain's offering. The Hebrew word for cultivate, one of the responsibilities given to Adam, can also be translated as either "work" or "worship." Cain's conversation with God indicates that he lost that distinction. Cain had a choice to "do well" (v. 7). He was warned that sin, the alternative, was nearby and had a "desire" (Hebrew *tesuqa*) for him, but he must "master" (Hebrew *mashal*) it (v. 7). These are the same words directed to Eve in Genesis 3:16 after her disobedience: "Yet your *desire (teshuah)* shall be for your husband, and he shall *rule (masal)* over you" (emphasis mine).

Cain, like his mother, failed to follow God and lift up his countenance; instead, he too put himself in the god-like position as giver and taker of life.

Another view, which I will expand in the third section of this book, takes Cain and Abel as types. Adam was a horticulturist. He sinned and incurred a curse on his means of production. Abel got outside of the curse by becoming a shepherd while Cain elected to live under the curse. Jehovah is about obedience and removing curses, and he was therefore indisposed toward Cain, who brought an offering as a point of pride to show what he could do under the curse.

We do not know Cain's intentions toward his brother. Did he mean to kill him, and plot to do so? Or did he simply have a temper and struck out without thinking? Cain had not seen death (at least of a human); was Abel's death thus a surprise? Cain had told Abel of God's warning, so they were still conversing prior to the attack.[33]

Genesis 4:7 is the first mention of sin in the Bible, and of several hundred uses, the only personification of it. Disobedience had resulted first in banishment from the garden; then, in the second generation, jealousy and fratricide. There was NO HOPE.

After the murder, God tells Cain that his brother's blood is crying out from *adamah*.[34] BUT GOD did not curse Cain. He was cursed from the ground (v. 11) and, much like Adam's punishment, *adamah* would not yield its strength to him. Further, Cain was to be a "vagrant and a wanderer on the earth *(eretz)*" (v. 12), but in fact he built a city (v. 17). The reason for the change can be inferred from Cain's response to God, "My punishment is too great to bear" (v. 13). The Hebrew word *avon* can mean iniquity or punishment of iniquity, and the sentence can be translated, "My iniquity is

homilies.

33. Gen. 4:8.
34. Gen. 4:10.

24

too great (to forgive)." He also seems repentant, realizing "from Thy *face* I will be hidden" (v. 14, emphasis mine). Cain protests that "You have driven me this day from the *face* of the ground (emphasis mine). That is the third mention of "face" (Hebrew *paniym*): Cain's countenance, the face of *adamah*, and God's face. He is to lose face-to-face contact with God and God's provision, *adamah*.

God not only protected Cain with a mark but relented and allowed him to settle down in Nod (which means wandering). That made Cain a Nodder, or wanderer, just as he was told in verse 12. We see the Divine sense of humor in play.

Cain built a city and named it after his son Enoch. Why a city-size group of people would help a man marked by God, and what the mark was, might come together in the speculation that the mark was leprosy. Leprosy in the Bible can be taken as the physical manifestation of sin. It starts small but insidiously progresses. It causes numbness and loss of pain as a warning, eventually causing loss of function and even loss of the whole limb. It disfigures. Lepers were outcasts, banished in Jesus' day to the valley of Gehenna[35]—a garbage gully with fires constantly burning and as close to hell as possible, and therefore a figurative equivalent for hell.

The city of Enoch could have been a leper colony. As such it was a refuge and foretold the cities of refuge in the book of Numbers.[36] Enoch would have had quite a legacy for a murder. Referring to the sevenfold vengeance to be taken on anyone who murdered Cain, his grandson Lamech boasted that he had killed men, and vengeance on his murderer would be seven times seventy,[37] the formulation that Jesus used to define how many times to forgive one's brother.[38]

(Note that the question of where did the people to populate the city come from fades away if we envision Adam as a subset of the creation of man in Genesis 1.)

God, in an ACT OF LOVE, gave Adam and Eve (who must have been devastated by the murder of Abel) another son, Seth, which means "in place of" (Abel).[39] The cycle ends, in similar fashion as cycle two, with a setting

---

35. The word is found in Young's Literal Translation.

36. Num. 35:25–32.

37. Gen. 4:24.

38. Matt. 18:22. Seventy was also the number of people Jacob took to Egypt and the number of nations in the Genesis 10 genealogy of Noah.

39. Gen. 5:4 states they "had other sons and daughters" besides Seth.

forward of the principles on which FAITH is to be built. In cycle three this is done via the genealogy which makes up chapter Five—a listing of the first ten men in the line descending from Adam toward the Messiah who was the thrust of God's plan and would be promised specifically later, as follows: Adam means "man." Seth was "put" (in place of) his murdered brother. He, rather than his older brother Cain, appears in the line from Adam to Noah and is the first in a line of younger-for-older switches. Methuselah (v. 22), famous as the longest-lived person in the Bible, has a name that means "when he dies something is going to happen" or, in the short version, "there shall come." The "something" was the flood. Genesis 5:29 tells us Noah means "give us rest." Adding the meanings for the remainder of the list preaches the Gospel: *Man* was *put* in an *incurable position,* but *praise be to God, there is One who will plead for us,* and *by initiation there shall come a powerful Overthrower who will give us rest.*[40]

The genealogies are not throwaway Scriptures.

Despite the redemptive message of Genesis 5, the sky started to darken again, signaling **cycle 4.** Genesis 6:22 states, "the sons of God saw that the daughters of men were beautiful; and they took them as wives." The "sons of God" were not angels (see Matt. 22:30 and 24:38-9), so there is the possibility that they are descendants from *adamah,* who intermarried with descendants of *eretz.* Whatever the case, "the wickedness of man was great on the earth." Worse, "every intent of the thoughts of [man's] heart was only evil continually" (v. 5). That is, purity (the sons of God) plus wickedness (the sons of men) equals wickedness. Therefore, God told Noah, "The end of all flesh has come" (v. 13). There was NO HOPE.

BUT GOD . . . told Noah to make an ark and gather animals. The ark was designed to stay afloat. It was not to go anywhere—it had no sail or rudder; it just had to ride the rough seas soon to come. God would direct it using wind and waves. It's worth noting that similar dimensions were used to make boats out of concrete when steel was scarce during World War II.[41]

Noah was in the tenth generation, the first who *could not* have known Adam, and the oldest who *could* have known Abram. Out with the old and in with the new with Noah (and the flood) as the turning point. Eight people entered the ark. Eight symbolizes new beginnings: the start of a

---

40. See Appendix C.

41. See concreteships.org for a history, names, and fates of these boats.

new week and the Festival of First Fruits[42] are on the eighth day, foretelling Christ's day-after-Sabbath resurrection. As the old spirituals tell, the waters of the flood washed away the old sin and were a type of the cleansing by the water and the blood to come: the washing by the water of the Word and the shed blood of the Lamb of God.

The events of the ark are misrepresented in children's Bible story books, a frequent source of Old Testament information and, unfortunately, misunderstanding. Noah and his family, a giraffe (always), and assorted other animals—wide smiles all around—are pictured waving from top of the ark. There are two problems with this scenario: no outer deck and no smiles. Everyone the eight people on the ark had known died in the flood. One reason they were 370 days on the ark was to allow time for decomposition of all the dead, bloated human and animal bodies floating in the water, and there were thousands of them.

The only way to avoid the total destruction of "every living thing that was upon the face of the land, from mankind to animals, to crawling things, and the birds of the sky,"[43] was to get on the ark; the only way through the door to salvation was to have a relationship with the one man who found favor with God. That has not changed.

There was a lot of water. The mountains everywhere were covered.[44] Save for the sun (initially blotted out by storm clouds) and the ark bobbing like a cork, it was back to Genesis 1:1. The sun would have warmed the water making currents that had no continents to contain them. The only situation like that now is the current that travels around Antarctica, the Antarctic Circumpolar Current. It is one of the most dangerous places on earth, with waves routinely sixty feet high. The solid surface below those currents would have been powerfully moved, eroded, packed, and sculpted. For dry land to appear again, the land must have pushed up in some places leaving deep troughs in others. The effect would have been large tsunamis that would have churned the undersea surfaces mightily, eventually settling into layer after layer. The coastlines which appear to have taken waves thousands of years to form might have been carved in a matter of days.[45]

42. Lev. 23:10.

43. Gen 7:23

44. Gen. 7:19.

45. A similar foreshortening of erosive timetables was seen on a smaller scale during the eruption of Mount St. Helens.

God caused a *wind* to pass over the earth, and the water subsided.[46] Wind (Hebrew *ruwach*) is the same word translated "Spirit" in Genesis 1:2: "and the *Spirit* of God was moving over the surface of the waters" (emphasis mine). God was making the earth good again.

After land appeared, vegetation began to grow once more, repeating the Genesis 1 order. Next, birds were sent out from the ark. One day a bird brought back an olive leave demonstrating that vegetation was again on the earth; then they stopped returning, showing they had found a place to live off the ark.[47] (This is a scene which is repeated in dealing with the cure of leprosy—a stand-in for sin, as we saw above—in Leviticus 14:7.)[48]

Then, continuing the creation order, all inhabitants exited the ark—animals first, then man.[49] God, in an ACT OF LOVE, promised never to curse *adamah* nor destroy every living thing again.[50]

Cycle 4 concludes with the FAITH-BUILDING Noahic covenant,[51] with the rainbow in the cloud as a sign and reminder of the covenant.[52] God accepted Noah's sacrifice (v. 21). A poetic section follows in verse 22:

While the earth remains,
Seedtime and harvest,
And cold and heat,
And summer and winter,
And day and night shall not cease.

As we have seen, the ark narrative is basically a second creation. The earth was again covered with water and dark. When God stopped the rain, the clouds separated, sunlight appeared, then dry land, then birds were in the air, then animals left the ark for the land, then Family Noah was established on the earth and planted another garden.

---

46. Gen. 8:1.

47. Gen. 8:6–12.

48. "He shall then sprinkle seven times the one who is to be cleansed from the leprosy and shall pronounce him clean, and shall let the live bird go free over the open field."

49. Gen. 8:7–12.

50. Gen. 8:21.

51. Gen. 9:9.

52. Gen. 9:13

Comparison of the events of the creation and the flood look like this:

Genesis 1	Genesis 2-11
Light (Kingdom)	Eden
Vertical separation (water)	Fall (separation from God)
Horizontal separation (land/water)	Cain kills Abel
Seeds	Genesis 5 genealogy of the Seed
Heavenly signs (sun and moon)	Rainbow
Birds	Dove with olive branch
Man	Family

Before proceeding, it is worth taking a moment to ask, "How do we approach apparently contradictory biblical passages?" We have already discussed Cain's punishment and the facts following his murder of Abel. In the flood narrative of Genesis 6–8, the years of man are given as 120.[53] In the genealogy of Genesis 11, many people lived longer than that. What to think? To conclude the Bible is in error is not the right answer. In 1 Peter 3:20 we are told, "the patience of God kept waiting in the days of Noah, during the construction of the ark." A consistent interpretation of the three passages is that God patiently gave man the 120 years of the ark's construction to repent. Most biblical "contradictions" can be resolved with enough study and thought.[54]

53. Gen. 6:3: Then the LORD said, "My Spirit shall not strive with man forever, because he also is flesh; nevertheless his days shall be one hundred and twenty years."

54. An unparalleled source of that study and thought has been done by rabbis over centuries and is collected in the Midrash (which means "study"). The Gemara and the writings of noted rabbis such as Rashi and Maimonides I also recommend. See www.alephbeta.org.

After the Ark, Trouble in Paradise (Again)

Genesis 9

Now these things happened to them as an example, and they were
written for our instruction.

1 CORINTHIANS 10:11

AS THE NINTH CHAPTER of Genesis starts, some things have changed after
the ark: all mankind has been reduced to the eight people coming off the
ark and then restarted with the three family lines of Noah's sons; in addition, animals were available for food for the first time (Gen. 9:3).[1] Some
things stayed the same: Noah was given Adam's blessing to "Be fruitful and
multiply, and fill the earth" (v. 1).

God's judgment may have "baptized" away old sin, but after the waters
subsided, new sin started almost immediately. Ham "saw the nakedness of
his father" while Noah was in a drunken stupor lying in his tent (v. 22).
We are told twice, in verses 8 and 22, that Ham was the father of Canaan.
That takes on meaning in verse 23 when Noah curses, not his son Ham the
perpetrator, but Ham's fourth son Canaan. Noah had started farming and
Ham had started having children in the same year. As it takes several years

---

1. "Every moving thing that is alive shall be food for you; I give all to you, as I gave the
green plant." In Gen. 7:2 God had said some animals were clean (and therefore the others
were not), but here all animals were food. The food laws would bring restrictions in Leviticus, but the post-flood "everything that moves" status would be reestablished in Acts
with Peter and the sheet from heaven. The Levitical restrictions were always temporary
and for educational purposes; their lessons are still valuable today.

to get the vineyard producing enough for wine, perhaps Noah was drunk celebrating the birth of Canaan.

The entire eighteenth chapter of Leviticus deals with incest. It warns against the practices of Egypt where the Israelites were coming from, and of the land of Canaan where they were going. The first example is verse 7, "you shall not uncover the nakedness of your father," which goes on to explain, "that is, the nakedness of your mother. She is your mother and you are not to uncover her nakedness." Perhaps Mrs. Noah was celebrating too.[2]

Canaan was Ham's fourth son, and his own fourth son was "the Amorite." The Amorites would be known for iniquity; indeed the Israelites would not come out of Egypt until the iniquity of the Amorite was *complete* (Hebrew, *kalah*).[3] The remedy for iniquity would come as Jesus of the tribe of Judah, Jacob's fourth son. With Noah being aware of what had happened when he sobered up, the unusual step of cursing a young grandson, and then given the biblical euphemistic use of "nakedness," it is at least possible that Ham did more than look. (He may have been celebrating a little himself.)

We have been seeing what has been called in other applications the King Lear paradigm. Shakespeare's Lear can be played either as a fool or as a tragic figure in uncontrollable circumstances, but the result is the same—at the end of the play Lear and his daughters are dead. If you want a different ending, changing your take on Lear is not enough—you must change the play. The Genesis "falls" are various attempts to change the players—Eve wanted to be like God, Cain like his brother, etc.—but always sin affected the same ending—NO HOPE.

The next attempted character change was the world's first get rich (or at least famous) scheme based on the latest technology: they had invented bricks. The Babylonians were going to do it right—burnt bricks with tar for mortar. There was nothing they purposed to do that was impossible.[4] Status became their god. So, God investigated, as he did in Eden and would do in Sodom. What he found was proud, evil hearts. There was no worry that the building would crowd God out of heaven, as brick structures cannot support weight much over ten stories; it takes steel (and elevators) to build

2. The rest of the chapter in Leviticus prohibits other incest, some committed by the patriarchs before the law was given. Interestingly, the one sexual relationship not mentioned as incest in Lev. 18 is between father and daughter, Lot's problem. The result of his incest was the Ammonites and Moabites, both enemies of Israel.

3. Gen. 15:16.

4. Gen. 11:6.

skyscrapers. In God's long view of history, a ten-story building is not much no matter how impressed the bricklayers were; a building with 164 floors was coming. We now fly so high into the heavens that their building would not even be visible.

The iniquity of the Babylonians was their crowding God out of their hearts by pride in the building. Babel's iniquity was just getting started, not "complete" as God would find in Sodom,[5] so his only punishment was to confuse their language and scatter them over the face of the earth. (This is another example of an event that parallels a previous story; in this instance Eden: hearts striving against God, the phrases "let us" see what is happening and "if we don't act," and finally relocation).

---

5. Gen. 18:21: *kalah* is usually translated as entirely or altogether in this verse.

Starting Home

Genesis 12

Now these things happened to them as an example, and they were
written for our instruction.

1 CORINTHIANS 10:11

NO HOPE IN A series of cycles is necessarily relative. For the people of Babel,
no hope wasn't the same as the no hope of the black watery lifeless nothing
of Genesis 1:2 or the storm-tossed watery flood of Genesis 7:19, but then
those two no hopes had their differences. Besides the obvious—the ark and
the sun—a marriage covenant was in place, and man had experience with
God to learn from. By the time of the no hope of the post-Babel diaspora in
(the current) **cycle 5,** the Noahic covenant was signaled by a rainbow, and
there were centuries of experience in God's ways to draw on. All of this was
cold comfort to the stockholders of Babel Brick and Tower, Inc., as they
stood on the Shinar plain trying to make themselves understood to people
suddenly speaking a hundred different tongues. There was NO HOPE

BUT GOD "said to Abram, go forth from your country, and from your
relatives and from your father's house, to the land which I will show you."[1]
Then God spoke WORDS OF LOVE to Abram: "I will make you a great nation,
and I will bless you, and make your name great." As he had done with Adam's start in the garden and Noah's fresh start coming off the ark, God gave
a blessing. This time, as Abram started home, God blessed all His people: "I

---

1. Gen. 12:1.

will bless those who bless you and the one who curses I will curse. And in you all the families of *adamah* shall be blessed."[2]

Who was Abram? From other sources, we learn more about him than his brief appearance in the genealogy of Genesis 11. In the book of Judith in the Apocrypha, Achior, the captain of all the sons of Ammon, tells the king that the Israelites' forefathers were of the Chaldeans:

> . . . and they sojourned heretofore in Mesopotamia, because they would not follow the gods of their fathers, which were in the land of Chaldea. For they left the way of their ancestors, and worshipped the God of Heaven, the God whom they knew; so they cast them out from the face of their gods, and they fled into Mesopotamia, and sojourned there for many days. Then their God commanded them to depart from the place where they sojourned, and to go into the land of Chanaan. [3]

There is more detail in the Midrash. According to rabbinical commentary, Abram's father had a house full of idols; he may have been a dealer. Abram realized they were false gods and smashed them. This put him at odds with Nimrod, the powerful regional ruler, who threw him into a fiery furnace. Like Daniel centuries later, he was protected and survived. Abram's brother, Haran, was also culpable but waited to see how it went with Abram before declaring whom he was with on the issue. When Abram came out of the fire unharmed, Haran declared with Abram. Nimrod then threw Haran (and his wife?) into the furnace; he (they?) perished. More on this later.

Earlier in a footnote I mentioned that we find many parallels between Abram and Gideon. Running afoul of the locals because of rejecting their gods is one of them.[4]

Flavius Josephus (AD 37–c.100), writing in *The Antiquities of the Jews*, adds of Abram that

> he was a person of great sagacity, both for understanding all things and persuading his hearers, and not mistaken in his opinions; for which reason he began to have higher notions of virtue than others had, and he determined to renew and change the opinions all men happened then to have concerning God; for he was the first that ventured to publish this notion. That there was but one God, the Creator of the universe; and that, as to other [gods], if they

2. Gen. 12:2–3.

3. *Jth.* 5:6-9.

4. Judg. 6:27.

contributed anything to the happiness of men, that each of them afforded it only according to his appointment, and not by their own power. [5]

Further, Josephus, quoting Berosus,[6] describes Abram as "skillful in celestial science" and states he taught the Egyptians arithmetic and astronomy, for "before Abram came into Egypt, they were unacquainted with those parts of learning."[7] Abram also was mentioned in histories and was the subject of a biography by Hectaeus.[8] We also know that he was wealthy, the head of a small but well-trained army, willing to take risks, patient and agreeable to delayed gratification, and "a man of incomparable virtue."[9] And he knew God's name.[10]

Abram also had one quality that separated him from other men and put him in a category with Enoch and Noah: he was willing to allow Jehovah to bring changes into his life—to be sanctified. As Oswald Chambers has noted:

> We take the term sanctification much too lightly. Are we prepared for what sanctification will cost? It will cost an intense narrowing of all our interests on earth, and an immense broadening of all our interests in God's point of view. It means every power of body, soul and spirit chained and kept for God's purpose only. Are we prepared for God to do in us all that He separated us for? And then after His work is done are we prepared to separate ourselves to God even as Jesus did?"[11]

Abram went forth from his homeland as he had been told. He did not know where he was going and he did not ask directions, making himself the prototype male driver. "Thus they came to the land of Canaan."[12] This is apparently important because it is mentioned three times in verses five and six. Abram was in someone else's land, they were home, and God did

---

5. Josephus, *The Antiquities of the Jews,* 1.7.1.

6. Josephus, *Antiquities,* 1.7.2.

7. Josephus, *Antiquities,* 1.8.2.

8. Josephus, *Antiquities ,* 1.7.2.

9. Josephus, *Antiquities ,* 1.17.

10. Gen. 12:8.

11. *My utmost for His Highest,* Feb. 8

12. Gen. 12:8.

not care—He gave the land to Abram's descendants.[13] God was BUILDING Abram's FAITH.

Abram responded by building an altar where God had appeared to him at Shechem, and another when he pitched his tents between Ai and Bethel. Ai means "pile of rocks," and the scene is a picture. Abram, called by God to separate himself from what he had known and to come to *adamah*, the promised land, worshiped God standing between a pile of rocks and Bethel, "the house of God," even as the church today is called to be separate and to be made from a pile of individual rocks into the house of God.

As **cycle 6** begins in Genesis 12:10, there is a famine on. Not quite NO HOPE, but Abram is definitely in a bind. He is new to the area and has no allies, no wells, and no resources. He also has mouths to feed: not just his wife, Sarai, and nephew, Lot, but also "persons which they had acquired in Haran."[14] He is also seventy-five years old. Abram had been promised the land, but there was no food in the land. There was food in Egypt, but he had never been to Egypt and certainly not with God. God called him to Canaan; could it be that Jehovah was the God of Egypt as well?

In Egypt, the worst of Abram's fears were realized as Sarai incited the local hormones and was hauled off to Pharaoh's harem. Abram seems to have been an accomplice—he had passed Sarai off as his sister. What was he doing?

We might take a step back and think through what we know about Abram. He left Haran without children at the advancing age of seventy-five with Sarai, his wife; not multiple wives as was within the custom of the day; not with concubines, not only a custom, but accepted in his family—his brother had a concubine.[15] We cannot assume that he didn't care about having a son, either. In the first conversation with Jehovah in which we are privy to what Abram said, his lack of an heir was the first thing he brought up.[16] He was out of Egypt ten years before Hagar came up.[17] It seems safe to assume that he wanted a son, and he wanted a son with Sarai. He was a one-woman man.

---

13. Gen. 12:7.
14. Gen. 12:5.
15. Gen. 22:24.
16. Gen. 15:2.
17. Gen. 16:3.

So, why did they try the "She is my sister" ruse? Well, first we know Abram and Sarai discussed the issue, and they discussed it early.[18] Both were convinced that locals would kill Abram the husband. Second, Abram appealed to Sarai for mercy: "this is the loving-kindness you will show me." He was not abandoning the marriage covenant; he was relying on it. Third, they were traveling through rough places in rough times. They had reason to think murder was a small thing to get his wife, even in Egypt where there was some rule of law. Fourth, if their assumption about local mores was correct, other deceits were no better. "She is my daughter" might have been believed but would not have kept Sarai out of the harem and would require a dowry to boot. "Friend" spares Abram but does nothing for Sarai. Conflicting stories (not that anyone was going to ask Sarai for information) was probably the worst potential danger of all—dealing wickedly with liars assuages all the local's (unlikely) qualms about murder. To give a little perspective to the problem they faced, consider the distances and difficult cultures they had survived, and think of the massive armies mustered for Helen of Troy—it's clear the couple managed fairly well. "Sister" worked most of the time.

There is more. In Genesis 20:12 Abraham tells Abimelech, ". . . she actually is my sister, the daughter of my father, but not the daughter of my mother, and she became my wife." The "daughter of my father" part may be a more expansive term than we think of today. Consistent with the times, this may be another example of how Bible genealogic lists are not necessarily as we expect today.

Commentary by the eleventh century Jewish scholar Rashi[19] can aid us here. He says that when Haran died in the furnace, his brothers, Abram and Nahor, took Haran's daughters as wives to raise up children for him to continue his legacy.[20] A similar act, taking the widow to wife, would be made part of the law centuries later and would get Judah in trouble before

---

18. Gen. 20:13.

19. Sefaria/Rashi on Genesis, page 1. Rashi Rabbi Solomon ben Isaac (Shlomo Yitzhaki), known as Rashi (based on an acronym of his Hebrew initials), is one of the most influential Jewish commentators in history. He was born in Troyes, Champagne, in northern France, in 1040. All editions of the Talmud published since the 1520s have included Rashi's commentary in the margins. His commentaries on the Bible have become a foundational element of Jewish education to this day. They are based on the Masoretic text, a version of the Bible compiled by scholars between the seventh and tenth centuries, in which they clarified pronunciation by establishing a vowel notation system.

20. Rashi on Genesis, Gen 11:28–31

that. Neither of the brothers took Haran's wife; perhaps she was dead, possibly dying with her husband. Considering the plight of single, fatherless women at the time, the brothers marrying their nieces was far and away the nieces' best course.

Whatever their reasons, Rashi says Nahor took Milcah, and Abram took Iscah. He says that Iscah was Sarai, noting that both names mean "Princess." Sarai may have been Abram's term of endearment for Iscah, assuming Rashi is right. As the story plays out with the grandchildren and great-grandchildren of Abram and Sarai, it seems they do not have a family tree so much as a family branch. More on this later.

Abram had been promised a great name and to be a great nation. He was told he would be a blessing to all the families of the earth. Sarai was a part of that. When she was taken to the harem there was NO HOPE.[21]

BUT GOD "struck Pharaoh and his house with great plagues" (Gen. 12:17). God did not seem to panic at all. He wanted Abram in Egypt, hence the famine. A type was being set.[22]

Gen. 12 and 13	ABRAM	Gen. 41–47 and Exod. 12	JOSEPH
10	Famine in the land	41:54	Famine in all the lands
11	Nearing Egypt	46:28	Nearing Goshen
11–13	Told Sarai what to say	46:34	Told his brothers what to say to Pharaoh
15	Sarai to harem	47:5	Brothers to Goshen
16	Given animals and servants	47:27	Acquired property and were fruitful
17	Plagues	Exod. 7-11	Plagues
19	Escorted out of Egypt	12:32	Told to leave Egypt
1	Lot with him	12:38	Mixed multitude
2	Very rich; livestock, silver, and gold	12:35 and 38	They had much livestock, silver, and gold

21. Unless God was provoking Pharaoh, something He would do when Israel was enslaved in Egypt, itself predicted long in advance (see Gen. 15).

22. For a more complete comparison, see John H. Sailhamer, *The Pentateuch as Narrative*, 142.

Deceived by the Blessings of God

Genesis 13

> Now these things happened to them as an example, and they were
> written for our instruction.
>
> 1 CORINTHIANS 10:11

As CYCLE 6 CONTINUES, Abram and Lot, having been escorted out of Egypt, traveled back to the friendlier surroundings between Bethel and Ai where Abram had built the altar earlier. Its utility complete, the famine had apparently ended; even so, due to Abram and Lot's Egyptian acquisitions, the land could not sustain all their herds (but did sustain Abram's greatly increased herds[1]). Furthermore, the Perizzites were now in the land.[2]

Abram, the beneficiary of God's generosity, in an ACT OF LOVE offered his nephew any land he chose. "[W]e are brothers[3]. . . please separate from me: if to the left, then I will go to the right, or if to the right, I will go to the left" (v. 9). Possibly Abram was being shrewd; maybe he had learned something about Lot during their travels. He had been promised all the land; now he was letting Lot choose a place to live, which was the very place Abram did not want—the valley of the Sodomites.

Lot, being deceived by what he thought was a rich land, chose the green valley of the Jordan, settling his tents near Sodom. The whole land

1. Gen. 12:16.

2. Gen. 13:7. Perizzites were Canaanite tribes. The name means "people of a village," so apparently the Canaanites had grown numerous enough to start living in villages.

3. Note that this is another example of condensing generations in speech.

39

of Canaan is small. There were few cities. They had to trade, if not directly with the people of Sodom, then with traders who had first-hand experience with them. Lot must have known what was going on in Sodom: "the men of Sodom were wicked exceedingly and sinners against the Lord" (v. 13). It *looked* like the garden of the Lord (v. 10), but he should have known it was not.

But, with the burden of his "blessings" from Egypt, Lot went for the green. He could have stayed farther north in the valley, but having just handled all that Egypt had thrown at them and come out the richer for it, little Sodom must have looked easy. He was wrong.

Abram also brought a surprise out of Egypt. Pharaoh "treated him well for [Sarai's] sake; and gave him sheep and oxen and donkeys and male and female servants,"[4] one of whom was probably the Egyptian, Hagar.

So, Abram settled in Canaan after Lot left. And in another FAITH-BUILDING promise, God said to him, "lift up your eyes . . . northward and southward and eastward and westward; for all the land which you see, I will give to you and to your descendants forever . . . if anyone can number the dust of the earth, then your descendants can also be numbered."[5] It is interesting, knowing (as Abram did not) how the story unfolds, that part of what he could see was the Jordan valley he had just given to Lot, who was not a descendant and therefore not part of the promise, but God honored Abram's promise to Lot.[6]

As Genesis 14:1 starts **cycle 7** with a regional conflict between kings from the north and the local rulers, we learn that Lot's progressively poorer decisions landed him in big trouble. Not only had he moved his tents closer to Sodom, he moved into the city. He then became part of the booty of the victorious kings heading back north. He was enslaved, impoverished, and had NO HOPE.

BUT GOD sent Abram. "Sent" should raise some objections because the text does not say that Abram was under God's instruction; but consider the whole picture. First, it is counterintuitive for Abram, at nearly eighty years old and with a group of only 318 men and a few Amorite allies, to go up against four battle-tested armies that had swept all before them. Second, he left his wife, his tents, and his flocks exposed to the surrounding

4. Gen. 12:16.
5. Gen. 13:14–16.
6. Deut. 2:19.

Canaanites and Perizzites. Third, the recent battles had destabilized the entire area: not only were there no powerful authorities left, but the survivors of their armies had fled to the hills[7] and now had nowhere to go (their cities had been looted and destroyed), living as roving marauders who survived by stealing and murder. Fourth, invasion by surrounding nations like the Egyptians and the Hittites, who must have been aware of the movement of four large armies and the recent events of the region, was a clear danger.

Fifth, his 318 fighting men had families, so Abram was responsible for at least a thousand lives in his own camp, a group too large to stay hidden in his absence. Sixth, by the time Abram learned of Lot's fate, the invading armies were as far away as Dan. (This last may have been an advantage.)

But "he led out his trained men."[8] The Hebrew word for "led" is *ruwq*,[9] which means emptied; in other words, he did not simply leave the camp poorly defended, he took everyone who could fight. Abram was either very reckless and a little suicidal—or he knew something.

Jehovah tells us in Genesis 26:5 that Abraham "obeyed Me and kept My charge, My commandments, My statutes and My laws." We also know from Isaiah 55:9 that "for as the heavens are higher than the earth, so are My ways higher than your ways and My thoughts than your thoughts." So, for Abraham to obey God, he had to have instructions to obey; he could not arrive at God's thoughts on his own. We also can see that most of that instruction occurred "off the record," and there are numerous examples of Abraham obviously having conversations with Jehovah that are not described in the text. I think this is one of those times.

God's ways in dealing with hostile nations eventually are recorded by Moses in Deuteronomy 20, but Abram knew them in Genesis 14. Whether from an on-the-spot crash course or previous training is unimportant to us now; we can see that Abram acted not impulsively, but instead, as Sailhamer points out,[10] his actions were exactly as God would instruct in Deuteronomy 20:1: "When you go out to battle against your enemies and see horses and chariots and people more numerous than you, do not be afraid of them: for the Lord your God who brought you up from the land of Egypt, is with you." Again, in verse 4: "The Lord is the one who goes with you, to fight for you against your enemies, to save you," And in verse 17 we

7. Gen. 14:10b.
8. Gen. 14:14.
9. *Strong's* H7324.
10. Sailhamer, *The Pentateuch as Narrative,* 147.

read, "You shall utterly destroy them." God also permitted using (literally *eating*) the booty in verse 14. More of Deuteronomy 20 comes into play when Melchizedek appears later in the chapter, but these events serve as a reminder that likely there were conversations between Abram and Jehovah to which we are not privy.

What we are told is that the battle between the nine kings took place in the valley of Siddim[11] south of what is now the Dead Sea, and that Abram "went in pursuit as far as Dan."[12] He was pursuing four armies of soldiers who were mostly on foot, had been on campaign for a while, had been in battle no doubt with wounded to care for, and who we are told were transporting booty and prisoners; in short, they traveled slowly. Abram, on the other hand, had only 318 troops of his own plus the Amorite allies—six hundred at most—and may have had horses, camels, mules, whatever. They could travel fast.

That is all we need to know about the rescue events; in other words, all the text tells us. We can, however, take a moment to speculate as to how Abram might attack four battle-hardened armies with only three companies of men.

Living in the rough, not to say, hostile environment to which God had led him taught valuable survival skills. His men were "trained."[13] Their environment forged them into a group of highly disciplined desert commandos, perfect for the job at hand. They attacked in a location over 160 miles from Abram's camp, so they had plenty of time to catch up to Chedorlaomer's army, scout his camps, and discover where the prisoners were and where the weaknesses existed. They had to find the best terrain for ambush and plan a night raid (or more likely many night raids), harassing Chedorlaomer from Dan all the way past Damascus to Hobah.[14] Every morning the soldiers would awaken to find more comrades killed in the night. Soon no one was sleeping, making matters worse for them. Scavenging parties sent out to look for firewood and food did not come back. By picking off the straggling units and those slowed by prisoners and booty, they were able to rescue everyone taken from Sodom as well as their possessions. The soldiers may have left the prisoners behind just to get away from the guerrilla attacks.

11. Gen. 14:10.
12. Gen. 14:14.
13. Gen. 14:14.
14. Gen. 14:15.

No doubt Gideon, who used the same tactics (split forces, attack at night, confusion) to defeat overwhelming odds, would use the stories of Abram and Deuteronomy to inspire his brave band of about the same size.

Traveling home, Abram is met by the kings of Salem and Sodom. Melchizedek, priest of *El Elyon*,[15] in an ACT OF LOVE brought sacraments and blessings. He acknowledged that God was Creator and therefore possessor of heaven and earth and therefore able to give improbable victory into Abram's hands. Deuteronomy 20:2 records that the priest informed the people before the battle that God would do this, but Melchizedek's priestly blessing again shows Abram's ties to the commands of God.

This is Abram's most public action showing his relationship with Jehovah. Until this point, he had built (private?) altars, called on the name of the Lord, and conversed with God, but we are told nothing of a public display.[16] The Melchizedek event, however, was beyond his backyard.

We know several things about Melchizedek. First, he was a king—of righteousness by his name,[17] and of peace (Salem). Second, he was priest of Most High God, so a priest *and* a king, a rare combination. Third, his was the order of Melchizedek,[18] not of Aaron. Fourth, he was without beginning or end, a priest perpetually, "made like the Son of God" (Heb. 7:3). To Melchizedek, a type of God's Christ, Abram gave a tithe (a thanksgiving peace offering to be set out in Leviticus).

The king of Sodom, in contrast, brought a business deal: Abram takes the spoils (they were already his by conquest), and the king takes the people (a king must have someone to rule). As openly as Abram accepted Melchizedek, he rejected the king of Sodom. "I have sworn ("lifted up my hand" in the ESV) to the Lord God Most High (he uses the more personal name), possessor of heaven and earth, that I will not take a thread or a sandal thong or anything that is yours, lest you should say 'I have made Abram rich'" (Gen. 14:22). This is another example of off-stage conversations between Jehovah and Abram. He does acknowledge a right to the spoils: using some, taking a tithe from them, and giving his Amorite allies their share. He was already rich but wanted to avoid the public appearance

15. Gen 14:18: *El Elyon* is Hebrew for God Most High

16. The present discussion is limited to what we are told in Scripture—what we "need to know." I have already quoted extra-biblical sources reporting Abram's public defense of God in Ur and Egypt. The point now is that we can we learn by implication based on biblical structure, inclusion, or exclusion.

17. Heb. 7:2.

18. Ps. 110:4 and Heb. 6:20.

of his riches having as their source anything but Most High God. Appearances had ruined Lot.

It is unclear when Abram made the declaration to God he described above—possibly on the journey back from battle. It is also unclear if "lest *you* make me rich" (emphasis mine) refers to the king of Sodom only, or if Abram had been at the altar at Ai, reflecting on the events of Egypt when Pharaoh gave him gifts ("you" in that case would mean "your kind"). Perhaps his faith and trust in God took an upward turn. His relationship was growing and became a source of courage for rescuing Lot and rejecting the king of Sodom. God Most High was his source of peace and protection. He had come a long way from Ur of the Chaldeans.

God responded in a FAITH-BUILDING vision: "Do not fear, Abram, I am a shield to you; your reward shall be great."[19] This probably provided a great deal of comfort and considerable faith building, considering that Abram had just done battle with a king campaigning to punish those who had crossed him and who could come back, and also that he (Abram) had just gone crossways with the neighboring rulers. Add to this all the aforementioned regional political/military situations, and it becomes abundantly clear that Abram had reason for fear. God knew all of this and responded in the way that would build Abram's faith the most—a promise of protection. Abram knew this would not be an empty promise, having seen God work against Pharaoh, who also possessed a mighty army, and most recently work against Chedorlaomer.

Cycle 7 had been big in Abram's growth and trust in God Most High, but big had only started.

19. Gen. 15:1.

No Hair and No Heir

Genesis 15

> Now these things happened to them as an example, and they were
> written for our instruction.

1 CORINTHIANS 10:11

ABRAM HAD HEARD PROMISES. He had been promised he would be a great
nation and have a great name;[1] he was promised that "all the land you
can see"[2] would be given to his offspring[3] and that they would be as
numerous as the dust of the earth.[4] Now he was being promised a shield
of protection by the God who had defeated Pharaoh of the south and
Chedorlaomer from the north.

Abram should have been a very contented man. He had it all: flocks,
money, war hero status, and a wife he loved. He was surrounded by faithful
men who would follow him into battle against all odds, and allies amongst
the inhabitants of the land. Most of the people of the valley owed him their
lives. Jehovah coming into his tent and promising protection and that "your
reward shall be very great"[5] should have been the cherry on his retirement
cake.

1. Gen. 12:2.
2. Gen. 13:15.
3. Gen. 12:7.
4. Gen. 13:16.
5. Gen. 15:1.

At the time he should have been the most content, he was not content at all. He was unhappy for the same reason that Jehovah had chosen him back in Ur, for the reason that he had been enticed to leave his father's house and go to a foreign land by a promise of being a great nation. Abram's focus was on eternity; his vision was beyond himself. He had what Twila Paris has called "forever eyes". Jehovah had picked a family man without a family.

To make matters more acute, Abram may have had what he considered an ace in the hole on the descendants front—Lot. If Abram remained childless, maybe Lot and Lot's descendants could be his lineage. According to Rashi, Lot was Sarai's brother, which explains why Abram took Lot with him on leaving Haran despite the instruction to "go forth from your country, and *from your relatives*" (emphasis mine). But now Lot had chosen to live in the Jordon valley a second time—this time with the king of Sodom whom Abram had just antagonized, so that avenue seemed to be closing.

The promises of a shield and a reward were vague, and their very vagueness gave Abram NO HOPE. **Cycle 8** starts as he expressed his discontent: "I am childless" (Gen. 15:2). The King James Version is stronger: "*Thou* hast given me no children" (emphasis mine). That was his heart. This is the first time we hear Abram speaking directly to Jehovah. Since the call came in Haran (or Ur), God has spoken and Abram has obeyed. Now Abram must speak.

What good are promises—great promises made by a great God—if they go only to "one born in my house"; that is, to the servant Eliezer (v. 3). He had stories to tell, experiences to share, and a faith to instill in a son's heart, but he had no son.

BUT GOD came to him in a word: "one shall come forth from your own body, he shall be your heir."[6] Then God took Abram outside (so the conversation had been going on in Abram's tent) and told him to *look* at the stars. Rashi cites the Midrash[7] explaining that "this word signifies looking from above downward;"[8] in other words, God wanted Abram to see the stars as He sees them.[9]

---

6. Gen. 15:4.

7. Genesis Rabbah 44:12

8. *Strong's* H5027 *hab-bet* per Westminster Leningrad Codex.

9. Which does pose the question, "When I see a rainbow, do I think of an effect of light refraction or of God's promise to Noah; when I look at stars do I see a collection of galaxies or think of God's prophesy to Abram?

Yes, there were thousands of stars, but he had already been promised numbers—when Lot moved to Sodom the first time, God had told Abram, "I will make your descendants as plentiful as the dust of the earth,"[10] and there is a lot of dust. "Count the stars, if you are able to count them."[11] The Hebrew word "count" is *caphar*.[12] It means to score, to recount (as a story, the usage in ninety percent of Old Testament occurrences), to make known or narrate, to tell, to celebrate; it is like our word cipher (number, calculate, code). The stars, which God placed as signs[13] (Gen. 1:14), tell a story, if you can decipher them. A different word is used in verse 6: "He *reckoned* (*chashab*)[14] it to him as righteousness," which is translated as "counted" in the ESV and KJV (changed to "accounted" in the NKJV; emphasis mine).

As mentioned earlier, Josephus gives Abram credit for introducing Chaldean astronomy to Egypt.[15] Abram was familiar with the stars and constellations. Could he decipher/recount God's story in the stars? Maybe. He would have been familiar with constellations that are visible to the un-assisted eye. He also would have been familiar with a particular band of twelve constellations known from ancient times as the zodiac. The zodiac is not astrology and horoscopes, although it has pretty much been co-opted by fortune-tellers and readers. In astronomy the zodiac is the constella-tions in a band nine degrees on either side of the apparent path of the sun around the earth—the ecliptic. The ecliptic differs from the equator by twenty-three degrees—the "tilt of the earth." The moon and solar system planets (known in ancient times as the "wandering stars") are all in the plane of the ecliptic.[16] Because of their brightness and movement in the sky, coupled with their apparent spatial relationship with the sun and moon, the occasional alignment or near alignment of the planets (and moon) were taken as omens and closely watched. The constellations in the sky behind them became markers as to where they were in the sky, and significance was placed on the constellations in the ecliptic—twelve (technically thir-teen) major constellations and many sub-constellations associated with the

10. Gen. 13:16.

11. Gen. 15:5.

12. *Strong's* H5608.

13. Hebrew *owth:* sign, omen, proof, indicator.

14. *Strong's* H2803.

15. Josephus, *The Antiquities of the Jews,* 1.8.2.

16. Mercury "wanders" more than the rest.

twelve. Additionally, each constellation has brighter stars that have names, adding greater detail and depth to the story.[17]

Unfortunately, astrology uses the same constellations. Someone thought the shapes or names of the constellations gave insight into a person's character based on the position of the constellation at the time of birth compared to where the stars are on a given day. Due to the wobbling of the earth's axis of rotation, a phenomenon called precession, there is a change in the alignment of the constellation through time, a shift of about one constellation every 2,000 years. So much for astrology. (They have a correction for precession, but the basic premise is all awattle.)

But the order of the constellations and the stories[18] they tell does not change.

As a further side note of interest, precession is in part responsible for the changes in climate that have transformed the Sahara from wetland to desert. This type of environmental change is necessarily on a multi-millennial time scale.

Genesis states that God placed lights in the sky "for signs and for seasons and for days and years."[19] Days and years are based on rotational and revolution speeds; seasons are set by whichever constellation appears on the eastern horizon at dawn; hence twelve "seasons," which later and more precisely (the constellations don't have clear starting and stopping points) were defined as months, and eventually even became vanity names for the powerful, such as Julius and Augustus Caesar.

A story can be found in the zodiac. Its constellations start with Virgo, the virgin, and proceed toward Libra, scales out of balance. Sagittarius the archer, a centaur with a dual nature, fights the Scorpion trying to sting him while the archer has his drawn bow pointed at the star Antares, the heart of the Scorpion. (Antares comes from anti-Aries; that is, anti-Christ). The story progresses around the ecliptic, ending with the victorious Leo, the lion, stepping on the head of Hydrae, the serpent. Various interpretations, some complex and involving the forty-eight sub-constellations, are subjects of articles and books. (See Appendix I, The Gospel Viewed in the Constellations.)

17. Amaral, *Story in the Stars*, 58–125.

18. Each constellation is a vignette with support from sub-constellations and named key stars more than a continuous narrative.

19. Gen. 1:14.

In beautiful poetical lines, the Scriptures describe the tapestry of the heavens:

> The heavens are telling of the glory of God;
> And their expanse is declaring the work of His hands.
> Day to day pours forth speech,
> and night to night reveals knowledge" (Ps. 19:1-2).

Adam gave names to all the animals,[20] but God named the stars. [21]

There's more:

> Lift up your eyes on high
> and see who has created these *stars,*
> The One who leads forth their host by number,
> He calls them all by name; Because of the greatness of His might and the strength of His power (Is. 40:26).

And this: "He counts the number of the stars; He gives names to all of them" (Ps. 147:4).

Perhaps God explained the unfolding story to Abram as each constellation became visible on the horizon. There is no time of year when all the constellations of the zodiac are visible—the sun is always between the earth and part of the ring of constellations because they are all on the same plane, obscuring different constellations throughout the year as the earth revolves around the sun. That is a small hill for a climber. Abram, the astronomer from Ur, would have been familiar with the unseen constellations.

No mention of constellations, much less the zodiac, is made in the Genesis 15 story. However, two things are clear. The first is that the stargazing took all night: Genesis 15:5 starts at night, and by verse 12 the sun is going down again. Counting backward from verse 12, Abram had placed animals for sacrifice as God directed. This required butchering three large animals, something that cannot be done quickly. We know his "house" included at least 318 fighting men. The men had wives; the wives had children. If they were Ozzie and Harriet with two children per couple, the total would have been over 1,200 people; if they were more like Jacob et al. (thirteen children), it would have been over four thousand—a small town. For health and odor reasons, the animals would have to be kept far off, each in a herd of its own kind.

---

20. Gen. 2:20.

21. Ps. 147:4.

God wanted three-year-old animals, not those of younger age kept near the tents to supply meat, nor older cows kept close for daily milk. The fact that He wanted a three-year-old heifer—a female that had not been bred—provides some useful information. A female that age that had not been bred, eaten, or sold implies she had been set aside for a purpose; that is, as a designated sacrificial animal. Jehovah specified that Abram bring his best animals. So, trips to the herds would have been necessary, which meant more time spent. Even with help (Abram is said to be driving the birds of prey off himself in verse 11—we do not know about the rest), preparation would have taken all day, ending as the sun went down again, so it is not unreasonable to assume the stargazing went on until the constellations were no longer visible at sunrise. Starting with constellations visible on the western horizon and proceeding east across the sky, and then adding new constellations as they appeared over the horizon until dawn would have included all the constellations visible at that time of year.[22]

Secondly, whatever happened *caphar*-ing the stars, Abram's concerns about an heir were relieved and resulted in one of the most remarkable verses in Scripture: "[Abram] believed in the LORD; and He reckoned it to him as righteousness" (v. 6). This is a paradigm shift, conjoining faith and righteousness. As familiar as Paul has made this to us,[23] it is the first use of the word *righteousness* in the Bible. We need to stop in the moment and consider what an amazing step forward this was, far eclipsing Neil Armstrong's first step onto the moon. The righteousness of God was imputed to man based on his faith by believing what God said was true. We should also consider that he did not just believe God about a verifiable fact—"Water flows downhill" or "That rock is hard"; he believed that God had a plan involving the whole earth, that it was far into the future, and that God would do what he had said. Further, and most important, the thing that Abram believed was about sons—his son in the near future and God's Son at some distant time known only to God. Righteousness comes only through faith in the Son.

The topic *immediately* turned to possessing the land: from verse 6— "Abram believed" about the son—to verse 7, "*and* . . . I will give you this land*," to verse 8— "*and* . . . how may I know that I shall possess it?" Abram

---

22. Probably fall if the four kings of the north started out in early spring and had time to fight their way as far south as Kadesh Barnea, then north against Sodom and Gomorrah, and then take the booty (slowly) back north of Damascus.

23. Rom. 4:3, 4:9, 4:22, and Gal. 3:6. James also quotes this verse in his epistle (2:23).

had previously been promised he would be a "great nation" (Gen. 12:2), the land would be given "to your offspring" (Gen. 12:7), "all the land that you see I will give to you and your offspring" (Gen. 13:14), and his offspring would be as "the dust of the earth" (Gen. 13:16). Abram had acted on these promises. He obeyed when he took his family, possessions, and herds on the long trip from Haran to an unfamiliar land. He had endured famine and hostile armies. But he had not *believed* until he was shown the stars (as evidenced by Abram's question to God about an heir in this chapter). He was not reckoned as righteous until he believed. All the above that he had done—and only a short reflection on what you would have to do to duplicate it will demonstrate how impressive were his works—had not resulted in him being reckoned by God as righteous. Nor would the event of Mt. Moriah make him righteous either as he was already deemed righteous by that time.

As Oswald Chambers has written, "We have to realize that we cannot earn or win anything from God; we must either receive it as a gift or do without it. The greatest blessing spiritually is the knowledge that we are destitute; until we get there Our Lord is powerless."[24]

Again, we do not know what in the stars made the difference, but we do know that the number of stars alone did not add anything to his information, that the question was specifically Abram's offspring, and that the answer he was given profoundly changed him. Realizing that God the Creator had placed the story of his descendants permanently in the stars, retold serially year after year, might have been the heart changer.

In this exchange between Abram and God, God makes two promises: descendants as the stars (v. 5) and "this land to possess it" (v. 7). Abram asked for a sign that he might know he would possess the land. He did not need to ask for a sign about his heir—he had the stars and could cipher them. In fact, he never wavered about the son, even when told he was to take him as a sacrifice to Mt. Moriah. (Hagar must be understood in the light of Abram having been promised a son "out of your [his] own body"— still vague and hard to interpret with a wife long past childbearing. It is only after Ishmael is born that God tells him, "I will bless [Sarah], and indeed I will give you a son by her"[25]).

---

24. Oswald Chambers, *My Utmost for His Highest*, Nov 28.

25. Gen. 17:16.

"Then he believed in the Lord; and He reckoned it to him as righteousness."[26] The statement is so foundational, it is quoted four times in the New Testament.[27] This is one of the four giant statements of the Pentateuch:

1. "In the beginning God created the heavens and the earth" (Gen. 1:1).

2. "Then he believed in the Lord; and He reckoned it to him as righteousness" (Gen. 15:6).

3. The Shema: "Hear O Israel, The Lord our God is one Lord. You shall love the Lord your God with all your heart and with all your soul and with all your might" (Deut. 6:4-5).

And the summary of the Pentateuch:

4. "I have set before you life and death, the blessing and the curse. So choose life . . ." (Deut. 30:19).

Creation. Faith. One Lord. Choose Life.

Then God continued with a WORD OF LOVE: "I am the Lord who brought you out of Ur of the Chaldeans to give you this land to possess" (v. 7). Having asked for a sign (as did Gideon), Abram proceeded, as discussed above, to assemble the animals for sacrifice according to God's request. Things seemed to be going well when an amazing chain of events took place, again, just off stage enough so that only the shadows can be seen. First, "birds of prey came down." The writer did not see their appearance on the scene of multiple dead animals as anything but expected: "*when*

---

26. Hebrew *tsdaqah:* rectitude, justice, virtue.

27. Rom. 4:3, a direct quote of the whole verse. The context, Rom. 4:2 and 5: "For if Abraham was justified by works, he has something to boast about; but not before God." "But to the one who does not work, but believes in Him who justifies the ungodly, his faith is reckoned as righteousness." Also, Rom. 4:22; context, Rom. 4:20–1: "with respect to the promise of God, he did not waver in unbelief, but grew strong in faith, giving glory to God, and being fully assured that what He had promised, He was able also to perform." And, Gal. 3:6; context: Gal. 3:5 and 7: "Does He then, who provides you with the Spirit and words miracles among you, do it by the works of the Law, or by hearing with faith?" "Therefore, be sure that it is those who are of faith that are sons of Abraham." Also, James 2:21–3: "Was not Abraham our father justified by works, when he offered up Isaac his son on the altar? You see that faith was working with his works, and as a result of the works, faith was perfected; and the Scripture was fulfilled which says, 'And Abraham believed God, and it was reckoned to his as righteousness' and he was called the friend of God."

the birds of prey came down"[28] (emphasis mine). Abram didn't either—he "drove them away."

Here another pause is needed in order to realize what is happening. When I drive down the highway and approach a roadkill, it is not unusual to see vultures or other large birds feeding on the carcass. I am impressed at how tenaciously they stay until the last possible moment as I come barreling at them, almost as if they expect me to slam on the brakes, jump out, and grab the carcass for myself. If they have not torn off some meat before I go past, sometimes I will see them in the rearview mirror already back at work. They are tenacious. Abram had a fight on his hands, especially for the turtledove and young pigeon,[29] which could be carried off whole. Further, we know there were several birds of prey and can assume they were presented with an opportunity of a lifetime with three large animals cut in half plus two birds all nicely laid out in rows.

It is not a stretch to imagine that Abram was busy. As he drove off one bird from the heifer, two landed on the ram on the other side. The more efficient he was at driving them off before they ripped off a morsel, the faster they came back when he was occupied elsewhere. He may have started out moving around the outside of the carcasses, but he would soon find his most advantageous position was in the middle aisle.

If that was the way the scene played out, Abram was in the midst of the sacrifices when "a deep sleep fell" on him (v. 12). Then terror (Hebrew *eymah:* fear) and great darkness fell on Abram as well. This was not the darkness of night; the sun was still going down. It can mean obscurity, misery, or the darkness of the grave. The same word is used in Exodus when the angel of the Lord went between Israel and the Egyptian army as a cloud and darkness.[30] In the darkness God tells Abram His plan for Abram's descendants: "Know for certain"[31] there will be four hundred years bondage, "Then in the fourth generation they will return here, for the iniquity of the Amorite is not yet complete."[32]

The sun set, and a smoking oven and a flaming torch passed between the halves of the animals laid out as God had commanded—right over Abram. This is tantamount to Abram's baptism: death on his right and

28. Gen. 15:11.
29. Gen. 15:9.
30. Exod. 14:19–20.
31. Gen. 15:13.
32. Gen. 15:16.

his left, God's covenant evoked, and the cloud of smoke and the flashing torchlight.

That brought together (on a small scale) all the elements that would be present at Mt. Sinai—darkness, cloud, thick gloom, smoke, fire, and the voice of God[33]—when God rescued Abram's descendants out of Egypt as He was then telling Abram He would, and again at the dedication of the tabernacle in the wilderness. Although these events were hundreds of years in the future, they are explicitly part of the promise God made to Abram on that day.

As Genesis 16:1 starts **Cycle 9,** Abram is eighty-five years old and Sarai is seventy-six. They have no children. The promise of an heir stands as "one who shall come forth from your [Abram] own body,"[34] a little vague at this stage of life for both. God had not mentioned Sarai. At some point they started casting about to see the promise fulfilled. All eyes landed on Hagar.

In desperation Sarai gave Hagar to Abram, much as Eve gave the apple to Adam. When Hagar became pregnant, something Sarai had been unable to do, Hagar despised her (v. 4)—not unlike the reaction of pride that Eve displayed when she produced a child.[35] The animosity and tension between the two women grew. Finally, Sarai delivered an ultimatum to Abram: her or me. What at first looked like the only hope became NO HOPE.

Hagar was Sarai's Egyptian maid. She may have been acquired in Ur or Haran or Canaan, but as she headed for Egypt when she needed help, she was probably acquired as a perk when Sarai was in the Pharaoh's harem. (Given to either Sarai as a handmaiden to assist with beautification, or to Abram as part of a bribe.) Harems were beauty cults loaded with hair stylists, cosmetologists, masseurs, and clothiers. The women were taught to walk and talk beauty. It was like a modeling school today. Hagar was in the middle of all that. As a handmaid there probably were few qualifications except looks.

Hagar was around Sarai most of the time that Abram was around Sarai, which means he saw her a lot. When the Sarai-Hagar relationship went sour (it seems unlikely Sarai would have given a maid she did not trust into her husband's arms), Sarai blamed Abram. This suggests the idea might have originated with him and that her request to "please go in to my maid"

33. Exod. 4:11–2.

34. Gen. 15:4

35. See earlier discussion on Genesis 3 in cycle 2.

(Gen. 16:2) was her acquiescence. "Abram listened to the voice of Sarai" because he wanted a son.

Faced with the prospect of the LORD judging between him and Sarai, Abram sided with Sarai, and the pregnant maid fled from the wrath of a woman scorned. BUT GOD returned her to her mistress with orders to submit (v. 9). However, He first comforted her with a WORD OF LOVE, explaining that her child was a son who would be named Ishmael and that the Lord "has given heed to your affliction" (v. 11). Ishmael was destined to live "to the east of his brothers" (v. 12), just as Adam and Eve set up shop east of Eden after their fall.

For her part, Hagar's FAITH grew as "I even remained alive here after seeing Him" (v. 13). The story of the angel and deliverance in the desert would become part of Ishmael's heritage.

Cycle 10 starts badly for Abram. Genesis 17 begins thirteen years after Genesis 16 ends, and while we cannot say there was no communication between Jehovah and Abram during that time, nothing we need to know passed between them. It was not only Jehovah giving him the cool treatment: Sarai put the blame for the falling out between her and Hagar squarely on Abram.[36] On top of that, the angel of the Lord recognized Hagar as "afflicted,"[37] a result of Abram having granted Sarai permission to drive out Hagar.[38] Clearly Hagar was not feeling overly charitable toward Abram herself. In thirteen years, no one got pregnant.

Ishmael was Abram's only comfort, but everyone had to be confused at Ishmael's role. God had sent Hagar back to give birth to Ishmael in Abram's house, but then . . . nothing. Thirteen years of nothing and Ishmael had grown to an age of accountability.

For Abram things had gone well in battle with the kings of the north. Things got better as he returned a hero greeted with Melchizedek's blessing, and better still in his response to the king of Sodom—God promised a great reward and sealed a covenant. Then he had the joy of the early part of Hagar's pregnancy knowing he would have an heir from his own body. Then . . . everything fell apart. Acrimony between Sarai and Hagar, Hagar leaving with the unborn heir, and tense months in camp waiting out the

---

36. Gen. 16:5.

37. Gen. 16:11.

38. Gen. 16:6: "you maid is in your power, do to her what is good in your sight."

rest of the pregnancy when she came back had to take its toll. That was followed by thirteen years of not knowing.

When God broke the silence, it was a stinging command: "I am God Almighty; Walk before Me, and be blameless."[39]

Abram knew who was blaming him—everyone. At least on a relative scale Abram had NO HOPE. BUT GOD made a new covenant. Several things changed. The covenant of Genesis 15:18 had said, "To *your descendants,*" but in Genesis 17:4, after Abram had fallen on his face before God acknowledging his errors and committing to walk blamelessly before *El Shaddai* (God Almighty), God said "My covenant with *you*" (emphasis mine).

Next, in an ACT OF LOVE, God changed Abram's name to Abraham. Exalted Father became Father of a Multitude. Abram had been promised a multitude of descendants before, but now he had God's imprimatur in his name. This was more than a nickname among friends; it was a seal of a covenant between unequals: God and man. It was like a man kneeling and a knight rising, his name changed to "Sir" as he was sworn to the king's service.

Sarai's name was changed to Sarah.[40] The name changes put further separation between the two covenants and brought Sarah explicitly into the covenant. Abram's (and Sarai's) mistake with Hagar had come from misunderstanding Jehovah's purpose in the marriage covenant. God told him "from your own body" an heir shall come, and they thought that must exclude Sarai. But God had said of marriage that "for this cause *a man shall leave his father* and mother, and shall cleave to his wife; and *they shall become one flesh*"[41] (emphasis mine). God's first command to Abram had been to "go forth . . . from your father's house."[42]

By way of BUILDING FAITH, and in the third distinction between the covenants of Genesis 15 and Genesis17, God added the covenant of circumcision. "This is My covenant, which you shall keep, between Me and you and your descendants after you: every male among you shall be circumcised."[43] Circumcision is the sign of the Abrahamic covenant even as the rainbow is the sign of the Noahic covenant.[44]

39. Gen. 17:2.
40. Gen. 17:15.
41. Gen. 2:24.
42. Gen. 12:1.
43. Gen. 17:10.
44. Gen. 9:12.

COVENANT	SIGN
Marriage	Leave father and mother (spiritual sense)
Noahic	Rainbow
Abrahamic	Circumcision

Some housekeeping takes place between the institution of circumcision and the next cycle. Importantly, as noted above, Sarah's name changed. Ishmael was also addressed: "As for Ishmael, I have heard you" (v. 20). Ishmael was to become the father of twelve princes.[45] The covenant of Genesis 15 included land from the Nile[46] to the Euphrates; Ishmael would get part of that, as would Esau and Lot's sons. The Genesis 17 covenant was not specific about land, but God is clear that "I will establish my covenant with Isaac" (v. 21).

Ishmael was "of Abraham's household" and circumcised with Abraham and the rest of the household,[47] and therefore he was not cut off as were the uncircumcised[48] and so did receive God's blessing. He was also not part of the covenant going forward. An interesting observation is that Abraham did not (or could not) produce his "only son"[49] until he was circumcised.

When Abraham was told he would have a son by Sarah, his heart's desire but a fallen dream, he laughed, whether from joy or amazement, or something less flattering we are not told. God did not let him forget, naming the son Isaac, meaning laughter.[50]

Soon everyone was laughing.

Cycle 11 examines the events of Sodom and Gomorrah from the perspective of the Mamre hillside (Gen. 18:16 through the end of the chapter), and cycle 12 (Gen. 19), from the valley.

The cycle starts as "the LORD appeared to Abraham by the oaks of Mamre, while he was sitting at the tent door in the heat of the day."[51] It seems that Abraham had not told Sarah that the LORD had told him that she would have a son, or, if he had, she did not believe him, possibly

45. Gen. 17:20.
46. Or the river of Egypt which was a smaller stream closer to Canaan.
47. Gen. 17:25.
48. Gen. 17:14.
49. Gen. 22:2.
50. Gen. 17:17–19.
51. Gen 18:1

attributing it as a tale for her husband to get back in her good graces. In any case, apparently tensions were still running high in the camp, because when the LORD appeared a ninety-nine-year-old man *ran* to meet him.[52]

Sarah is told of the impending pregnancy, but it is not to start right away. Several events—three of our cycles in fact—were to intervene and thus require our attention.

Cycle 11 continues as God and Abraham are walking together leaving Abraham's tents on the trail down into the Jordan valley. The outcry from the valley had been great, and Sodom and Gomorrah have NO HOPE. BUT GOD decided to share his plan with Abraham because he was "chosen . . . that he might command his children and his household after him to keep the way of the LORD by doing righteousness and justice"[53] and because "in him all the nations of the earth will be blessed."[54] Commanding justice requires training.

When exploring Genesis chapter 3, we posited the view that what Jehovah and Adam were discussing on their evening garden strolls was the knowledge of good and evil. God's intention was to train Adam. Now Abraham stood in Adam's stead. He had failed his own Tree-of-the-Knowledge-of-Good-and-Evil test when Sarai offered him Hagar, but instead of hiding when called on it, Abraham ran toward God. Now they were walking together, and God took up the discussion where it had been dropped—how to deal with evil.

First, God would check the facts. Second, whatever the unrighteousness and injustice level is, "I will know" (v. 21). The term "God knows" has become such a casual and loosely used phrase that the spiritual reality is lost. In dealing with Sodom, in teaching Abraham, and in setting standards of justice, God was not casual. The cry from Sodom (the land) was like the cry of Abel's blood from *adamah*,[55] the cry for justice. God would know if "they have done entirely according to its outcry."[56] The Hebrew is "they have made a complete end," similar to the wickedness of the Amorites being complete before Israel comes out of Egypt.[57] The facts showed Sodom's iniquity was complete and the inhabitants were destroyed, as the Amorite

---

52. Gen 18:3
53. Gen. 18:19.
54. Gen. 18:18.
55. Gen. 4:11.
56. Gen. 18:21.
57. Gen. 15:16.

would be nearly five hundred years later when their sin was complete and Israel was delivered from Egyptian bondage. Importantly, Jehovah was willing to subject His chosen people to four hundred years of slavery off the land rather than expose them to the iniquity on the land. Given the Egyptian pantheon of gods and other practices, the Amorites must have been wicked indeed.

The conversation *seems* to turn on numbers, but it does not. Starting with fifty righteous souls in Sodom, a number both God and Abraham knew was improbable, and tightening the requirements down to ten, Abraham had done nothing to save his four righteous relatives in Sodom. It would have done no good to progress below ten—he already knew the answer: eight righteous people did not stop the destruction of Noah's world.[58]

The conversation was Abraham's ACT OF LOVE toward the righteous of *adamah*.[59] Giving him credit for not thinking that God needed reminding that Lot was in Sodom, he was, in effect, asking what would happen to "righteous Lot,"[60] as Peter calls him. As with Noah, destruction would cost the righteous everything they owned, even if God spared their lives. To BUILD FAITH God discussed justice when the righteous live amid the wicked. When can a few saints intercede to avert judgment on the "whole place?" When does God move the saints to safety?

Cycle 12 begins in chapter 19 as the angels arrive in Sodom. The acts of wickedness by all of Sodom, young and old and from all areas of the city, quickly demonstrate there is NO HOPE for the valley. In a dramatic confrontation between Lot and his neighbors outside his front door, they threaten the angels and then Lot himself. After the angels strike the mob blind, pull Lot inside, and "shut" the door, the mob even though blinded still try to get at their intended victims. They "wearied themselves trying to find the doorway" which had been right in front of them.[61] The word "shut" is the same as when God closed the door of the ark.[62] It literally means healed, the same word used in Genesis 2 when God took a rib from Adam and

58. Lot's family might have numbered ten. It is unclear how many daughters Lot had. One reading of 19:12 suggests he had two daughters married and two betrothed. He also had sons. Counting sons-in-law (2), daughters (4), sons (2), plus Mrs. Lot, Lot's household was possibly as many as ten.

59. Gen. 19:26: God overthrew all the inhabitants and what grew on *adamah*.

60. 2 Pet. 2:7.

61. Gen. 19:11.

62. Gen. 7:16.

"closed up" his side.[63] The men of Sodom could not find the door because there was no door—the doorway was healed over. Their pounding on the wall was like the pounding on the wall of the ark as people panicked with the rising of floodwaters. Judgment was imminent. The persistence of the Sodomites, despite having been blinded by the angels, testifies to the depths of their depravity.

Lot gives his sons-in-law the opportunity to flee Sodom[64] with him, but they think he is jesting. The wicked always think God is jesting. The angels asked him about sons, but he made no attempt to warn sons. It seems unlikely the angels would not know whether he had sons or not, so Lot might have already given up on his sons as lost to the lusts of Sodom.

BUT GOD tells Lot to flee with his family and any disciples,[65] and in an ACT OF LOVE the angels literally grab them by the hand and lead them away. Despite the dire warnings and urgent actions of the angels who are clearly saving his life, Lot does not want to "escape to the mountains."[66] His excuse was that "the disaster" would overtake him if he fled to the mountains "and I die." Lot could not have been concerned about the extra time it would take to climb the mountain during the crisis because he was told the angels could "do nothing until you arrive" at the haven.[67] "[T]he disaster" Lot feared is *ra* in the Hebrew. It means "the result of the inability to come up to good standards which will benefit."[68] It is the opposite of what God spoke over Abraham, "to keep the way of the Lord by doing righteousness and justice."[69]

That was the rub. Lot could not go into the mountains because of who was there. The Canaanites were there. They might kill him as a refugee of God's judgment in the valley. But mainly Abraham was there. "And I die" can mean literally or figuratively. Lot could not bear to face Abraham, who had already rescued him once and who had given him his choice of all the

---

63. Gen. 2:21: "then He took one of his ribs, and closed up the flesh at that place."

64. Sodom means "burning"; Gomorrah, the site now under water, means "submersion."

65. Gen. 19:12. *Strong's* H1121: *Ben*: son, disciple. We are not told Lot had sons, but he might have had a positive influence on some of the people of Sodom.

66. Gen. 19:17.

67. Gen. 19:22.

68. *Strong's* H7451.

69. Gen. 18:19.

land. Now Lot had lost all his herds, servants, wealth, and wife. He would die if he had to face Abraham. He chose a cave instead.

Famously, Mrs. Lot looked back at Sodom and was judged by salt, which represents purity and imparts protection from rottenness (think salt pork and long-term storage). Chapter 19 is the only mention that Lot had a wife, even though Lot is mentioned leaving Haran, going in and out of Egypt, moving to the valley to separate his herds, and being rescued from Chedorlaomer. He may have married a woman of the valley. That would explain why she was drawn to look back as her home and family were perishing.

He did have his own life and the lives of his daughters. This was the result of God's FAITH-BUILDING ACT of remembering not Abraham's words or arguments, but remembering Abraham himself.[70] (Hebrew *zakar*: to remember, to think on, even as God "remembered Noah" in the ark[71]—not someone he had forgotten, but whom he was thinking on for good.)

Two historical notes: Josephus, writing in the first century AD, states that he had seen the pillar of salt that was the result of Lot's wife looking back at Sodom. Clement of Rome, a contemporary of Josephus, also attested to seeing it.[72]

The town of Zoar was spared because of one righteous man. The Israelites in the desert were spared because Moses would not move but were judged individually later. There is no formula. God told Moses, "I will have mercy on whom I have mercy, and I will have compassion on whom I have compassion."[73]

Lot's incestuous acts of fathering the Moabites and the Ammonites with his daughters demonstrated the daughters' understanding of how hopeless and ashamed their father felt. The assistance of Uncle Abraham was not far away in distance, but they perceived an impassible moral gulf between their father and his uncle leading to desperation. That they had to get their father drunk is good evidence that he would not have countenanced the plan otherwise.

Despite his mistakes and misadventures, Lot protected the angelic visitors who presented to the gates of his city. In the end he is called righteous

---

70. Gen. 19:29.

71. Gen. 8:1.

72. Josephus, *Antiquities*, 1.11.4.

73. Rom. 9:15.

by God;[74] his incestuous offspring are not. When Ehud was judging Israel, "the LORD has handed your enemies the Moabites over to you . . . They struck and killed about ten thousand Moabites at that time, all robust and valiant men; and no one escaped."[75] Both David[76] and Jotham[77] defeated the Ammonites in battle.

As **cycle 13** begins in Genesis 20:1, we are back at Abraham's camp overlooking the valley. Abraham had moved to Mamre when Lot left for the valley. Most of ten years passed before the Hagar incident, and Ishmael was now thirteen, meaning Abraham had lived in Mamre twenty-three years. Abraham had also been promised that Sarah would soon become pregnant—more reason to circle the wagons where they were. But when he walked out to the bluff overlooking Sodom early the next morning and saw the smoke rising like out of a furnace, and saw the destruction, and smelled the burning flesh, he moved.[78]

Trouble immediately ensued; it was déjà vu all over again.[79] He settled in Gerar. Gerar had a king and the king had an army—Egypt redux. Abimelech was the title for the king of the area, just as Pharaoh was the title for the ruler of Egypt. A special title was not the only thing the two kings had in common. Sarah had managed the twenty-three years well it seems, the brother-sister pact was still in force, and the results were the same as Egypt. Sarah was haremed. On the surface it seems that the present account is a repeat of the other. As we shall see, there are more differences than similarities.

No mention of Sarah's beauty appears in Genesis 20, leaving the possibility that Abimelech was only practicing Middle Eastern diplomacy by "marrying" Abraham's sister. But Sarah had turned heads in Egypt, a place that was used to beautiful women. She would also live another twenty-eight years after these events in Gerar. Head-turners are usually still attractive twenty-eight years before their deaths. Not to mention that taking the desert chief's sister hostage is a poor form of diplomacy even by Middle Eastern standards. Further, Abimelech demonstrated his diplomatic skills

74. 2 Pet. 2:7.
75. Jdg. 3:28–29.
76. 2 Sam. 10:6–14.
77. 2 Ch. 27:5.
78. Gen. 20:1.
79. Yogi Berra.

in the next chapter, with much better results.[80] All things considered, hormones were likely in play.

The clock was ticking on God's promise of a son: "I will certainly return to you at this time next year; and behold, your wife Sarah will have a son."[81] A nine-month pregnancy left three months before impregnation. Now Sarah's was in Abimelech's harem and "the LORD had completely closed all the wombs of the household of Abimelech."[82] It would take time—weeks—before it became clear that no one was getting pregnant. Sarah's situation was such that confusion about parentage was a definite possibility. Abraham was back to NO HOPE.[83]

BUT GOD came to Abimelech in a dream of the night.[84] The dream started innocently enough: "You are a dead man." Abimelech did what anyone else would have done in that circumstance—he blamed someone else; namely, Abraham and Sarah. God reasoned with Abimelech, something he did not do with Pharaoh. Whereas the plagues God used in Egypt to extract Sarai from the harem were types of the plagues of Exodus that would be judgmental, the affliction of Abimelech and his house were in fact an ACT OF LOVE to keep him from sinning *against God*.[85] This last had to get Abimelech's attention.

The rest of the story does not fit modern Western sensibilities. Apparently, the problem was not that the king had forcibly taken a woman into his house because she excited him sexually, but only that she was married. The fact that Abraham and Sarah had misled Abimelech about her marital status was treated by Abraham and by God as a technicality. Abraham even ends the story wearing a white hat.

---

80. Gen. 21:22.

81. Gen. 18:10.

82. Gen 20:18.

83. Or maybe not: after his experiences in Egypt, Abraham may have just been waiting for the fireworks. If he was that confident in Jehovah's protection, one would hope he would have abandoned the sister ruse entirely, but the way things went certainly strengthened his hand concerning Abimelech. This continues to be the weak link in our understanding of the relationship between Abraham and God. The idea that Abraham was operating on instructions from God, who may have been seeking cause to discipline Pharaoh and Abimelech, never entirely goes away.

84. Gen. 20:3.

85. Gen. 20:6: Then God said to him in the dream, "Yes, I know that in the integrity of your heart you have done this, and I also kept you from sinning against Me; therefore I did not let you touch her."

The story continues with Abimelech confronting Abraham (as did Pharaoh). Before the plagues in Egypt, Abraham had been given gifts and was treated well, a bribe of sorts. Money was coming from Abimelech but with the purpose of vindicating Sarah (and therefore Abimelech).

Abraham's defense was that Sarah was in fact his (half-) sister. There are possibilities. The first is that Sarah was Terah's daughter by a wife other than Abraham's mother. Another follows Jewish tradition and the account by Josephus[86] and also Saint Jerome that Sarah was the daughter of Abraham's brother Haran, the sister of Lot and Milcah, and either was the same as Iscah (Matthew Henry) or her twin sister (Saint Jerome).[87] When Abraham told Abimelech about Sarah saying that "she actually is my sister, the daughter of my father, but not the daughter of my mother, and she became my wife,"[88] he may have been referring to his elder brother[89] as a father-type whom he revered.

As Nahor, Abraham's other brother, also took as wife a second of Haran's daughters (Milcah), the family tree is narrow indeed: more a palm than an oak. Sarah's son Isaac married her sister's granddaughter Rebekah, who was also the granddaughter of Abraham's brother, a double great niece. That narrowed the lineage further: the family limb.

Abimelech gave presents and silver to vindicate Sarah, gifts that were extremely important, as she would soon become pregnant. Abraham accepted the presents, in contrast to those offered by the king of Sodom in cycle 7, because of their significance relating to Sarah. Then, in his own vindication, God's prophet Abraham prays for Abimelech, who is healed.[90]

Easy as it is to criticize Abraham for acting selfishly to save his own skin while putting Sarah at risk, God does not seem to be bothered at all. He has no problem with the fix, uses the predicaments to His own purposes,

86. Josephus, *Antiquities,* 1.6.5.

87. Gen. 11:29.

88. Gen. 20:12.

89. Who was older, Abram or Haran? In the Gen. 11 genealogy Abram is mentioned first, but these are not always in order. Gen. 12:1 starts "now," implying it happened right after the end of Gen. 11. Gen. 11:32: Terah died at 205, Abram was 75 making Terah 130 at Abram's birth. Terah's first child was born when he was 70. Haran then would have been 60 at Abram's birth and 70 when his daughter Sarai was born—if Josephus is correct.

90. Gen 20:17 That Abimelech needed to be healed shows that God had done more than close wombs and helps us better understand how the time urgency problem discussed above was handled—possibly a herpes-like plague.

declares Abraham a prophet—the first in the Bible, and, for all we know, He might have told Abraham to describe Sarah as his sister when He called them out of Haran. St. Chrysostom may have had Abraham and Sarah in mind when he wrote, "the extent of the Lord's inventiveness: when He allows terrible things to reach a climax, then it is that in turn He scatters the storm and brings peace and quiet and a complete change of fortunes so as to teach us the greatness of His power."[91]

In judging Abraham, we may be confusing selfishness with humility. Montesquieu has pointed out that the principle men call "honor" is at opposite poles to the principle of biblical religion.[92]

Interestingly, neither deception nor fear of being murdered is condemned in other biblical stories. David pretended insanity[93] and Rahab lied;[94] Elijah ran from Jezebel.[95] Certain situations exist where the moral imperative seems to condone a lie: harboring Jews with Nazis at the door or law enforcement using undercover agents, for instance. In any case, we should probably hesitate to condemn what God does not.

Before moving to the next cycle, let us take a moment to consider a recurrent theme of Genesis. Abimelech states that he and his kingdom were experiencing *a great sin*[96] (Hebrew *chata'ah*, meaning sin or sin offering[97]). The same word is used by Moses after Aaron forged the golden calf.[98] Who did Abimelech sin against? Not God (v. 6); certainly not Abraham or Sarah (v. 5). Further, God acknowledges that Abimelech acted "in the integrity of [his] heart." The problem Abimelech had was that the integrity of his heart—the customs of the day, the way things were done—did not meet standards set in creation, what is commonly referred to as natural law.

We have already had cases of actions transgressing natural law that resulted in an outcry of creation: Abel's blood cried out to God from *adamah*,[99] the building at Babel drew God's attention, the cry from Sodom

---

91. St. John Chrysostom, *Homilies of Genesis* 18-45, 273.

92. Pangle, *Political Philosophy,* 139.

93. 1 Sam. 21:10–15.

94. Jdgs. 2

95. 1 Kings 19:3.

96. Gen. 20:9

97. *Strong's* 2401.

98. Exod. 32:21.

99. Gen. 4:10.

was great.[100] Even without a written code of conduct or a book of laws, man is held to account by natural law which he is expected to discern from the creation and creation's God:

> For the wrath of God is revealed from heaven against all ungodliness and unrighteousness of men, who suppress the truth in unrighteousness, because that which is known about God is evident within them; for God made it evident to them. For since the creation of the world His invisible attributes, His eternal power and divine nature, have been clearly seen, being understood through what has been made, so that they are without excuse (Rom. 1:18–20).

Treating women as sexual chattel is an offense to natural law even if it is common practice in any given time and locale. Most instances seem left unpunished to the non-discerning. Natural law is made visible only when we study the creation closely. God's eternal power and righteousness are invisible; nevertheless, transgressors of the natural order are "without excuse." The Bible never condemns slavery, which is a type for sin. Indeed, part of the settlement between Abimelech and Abraham was male and female servants.[101] However, sexual intercourse is part of the marriage covenant; thus sexual slavery transgresses natural law.

The cycle ends with a FAITH-BUILDING ACT:

> Then the Lord took note of Sarah as He had said . . . so Sarah conceived and bore a son to Abraham in his old age, at the appointed time of which God had spoken to him. Now Abraham was one hundred years old when his son Isaac was born to him. And the child grew and was weaned, and Abraham made a great feast on the day that Isaac was weaned.[102]

Despite that happy note, **cycle 14** begins in Genesis 21:9 and, as always, with NO HOPE: the conflict between Sarah and Hagar grew to include Abraham's son Ishmael, whom Sarah saw mocking Isaac. The smugness of Hagar and her son suggests the attitudes of Eve and her son, Cain, who were also driven out (of Eden and before the face of God, respectively).

Sarah demanded that Abraham drive away Ishmael. Abraham was understandably in great distress because of his son. "BUT GOD comforted

---

100. Gen. 18:20.

101. Gen. 20:14.

102. Gen. 21:12, 5, 8.

Abraham.[103]" Promises of safety and prosperity for Ishmael are given, but only Abraham considers Ishmael his legitimate son. To Sarah and God, he is "the son of the maid,"[104] and God is explicit that Abraham's descendants would come only through Isaac.[105]

Characteristically, Abraham does not delay. He rises early and sends Hagar and Ishmael away. The story does get a bit strange at that point, however. Abraham gives Hagar only bread and water as he turns her out into the desert. Then Ishmael, at least fourteen years old and having lived in the area his whole life—Ishmael who should have been "desert smart"— grows faint and is left under a bush crying. Depression seems likely.

This time Hagar was headed for Arabia[106] instead of Egypt. She was aware of the prophesies and assurances concerning her son.

The angel of God sizes up the situation and gets right to the point: "What is the matter with you?"[107] The question is addressed to Hagar, but given that she and Ishmael are sitting under trees in the desert a hundred yards apart, and both are crying, he probably meant both of them. The answer seems to be that a decade and a half of being the apparent heir born to an elderly father had resulted in a spoiled child who now had to be taken by the hand as his fortunes suddenly deteriorated, not totally beyond understanding and certainly not beyond God's LOVE. God opens their eyes to a well they had not seen[108] and they were revived. Their FAITH is bolstered by a promise of becoming a great nation. Ishmael apparently lived happily ever after and did return to help Isaac bury their father Abraham many years later.

The types in the Pentateuch are complex, and we have not spent much time with them, as we have been looking at the recurrent cyclical design of the narrative—and types will be looked at more closely in Section 3— but a brief venture into typology is warranted (at least according to Paul, who studied the matter).[109] Abraham had two "wives" and had a son by

---

103. Gen. 21:12.

104. Gen. 21:10, 13.

105. Gen. 21:12.

106. Gen. 21:21.

107. Gen. 21:17.

108. Possibly due to bitterness, just like the Israelites could not drink the waters of Marah in Exod. 15:23, "for they were bitter." "They" could refer to the people as easily as the water.

109. Gal. 4:22–31

each. Ishmael was the son of the bondwoman, a product of Abraham's (and Sarah's) attempt to fulfill a promise that God had made and God intended to fulfill. Ishmael looked like the son of promise: he was circumcised, he was trained by Abraham, he lived in the camp with the people of God, he sat around the campfires at night and heard the stories. For thirteen years he passed as the real thing.

Imagine visiting Abraham just before cycle 14. He would introduce his two sons (and maybe Sarah). His camp would look like any other camp you might have visited in the area: daily chores getting done, all the children playing, meals being cooked. You would not likely notice a difference in the relationship between Abraham and his sons.

Isaac, however, was the son of the freewoman—Abraham's son of faith and his "only son"[110] from God's perspective. Abraham's relationship with Sarah is analogous to the relationship between Christ and the church, His bride. His relationship with Hagar is different in all ways except it produced a son. For instance, God did not consider them "one flesh" and allowed her to be driven out.[111]

Paul sees these two types as two covenants that have important applications for us as believers. I produce daily life "fruit." Some of the produce is without faith from the bondwoman in me and is like Ishmael—it looks good and has a religious flavor, but it is not the product of faith and belief. Other produce comes out of faith from the freewoman in me—the real fruit that will not burn away.

To tell the difference between Ishmael and Isaac I must know God's heart; to know my own heart, I can look at the fruit I am producing and compare it to God's standards.

Starting in Genesis 21:22, **cycle 15** lacks the drama of the other cycles and draws attention mainly in the form of "why is this part included?" When Abimelech showed up with his general (who probably showed up with his army), Abraham might have considered that Abimelech was having second thoughts about how their last encounter went and wanted revenge. After all, the king of Shechem was out a lot of money and had personally been compromised. On the other hand, NO HOPE should have become more manageable with each cycle as Abraham experienced God's faithfulness and power, His love, and His faith-building plan.

110. Gen. 22:2.
111. Gen. 21:12.

Abraham could have been facing a tight situation, as there had been disputes about wells between the two men's herdsmen, BUT GOD had impressed Abimelech mightily. Abimelech was there to arrange his own peace with Abraham (and Abraham's God), not to demand tribute or blood. This, Abraham granted and willingly settled the dispute in an ACT OF LOVE by giving Abimelech gifts. He initiated the covenant of Beersheba in an ACT OF FAITH by setting aside seven ewes[112] as a witness (Hebrew *edah,* a noun only used to denote permanence[113]) of the oaths taken—presumably by God, as that is what Abimelech wanted.[114] Abraham called on *El Olam,* a name of the Everlasting God denoting might as a sign of God's protection in the presence of (potential) enemies. The name denotes presence in the past and future.

Abraham made shrewd use of covenant. His well was lost. He had no deed. If he seized it, he would have to constantly defend it and could lose it again. At a cost of seven ewes, he repossessed the well in a way it could not be lost—by covenant with Abimelech himself.

We see a progression: Abraham leaving Haran at God's direction, fulfilling his father Terah's plan to go to Canaan;[115] becoming the minor partner in a covenant with Jehovah while in a "deep sleep" with the torch and smoking oven passed between the offerings he had prepared as God had directed;[116] and now entering a covenant on God's behalf as His representative and designated prophet, setting aside symbolic animals of his own choosing.

The progression had not been smooth. Hagar had been a blind alley, but Abraham had backed out of it and allowed Sarah satisfaction. Ishmael was a hard lesson and a painful parting, even if mitigated somewhat by the presence of Isaac. Again, God's advice was to follow Sarah's wishes. Although the genealogies are almost exclusively male and the stories are mostly about men, we are usually shown the wives' influence: Eve with the fruit, Sarah with Hagar, Rebekah mirroring Sarah, and Rachel managing Jacob's sleeping arrangements and orchestrating the Jacob/Esau switch.

---

112. The Hebrew words for "seven" and "oath" are similar, and a word play is probably intended.

113. See Josh. 24:27.

114. Gen. 21:23.

115. Gen. 11:31.

116. Gen. 15:17.

The road from Haran had been ups and downs—mostly ups but some precipitous downs, with one lasting thirteen years.

Abraham's relationship with Jehovah had grown through an understanding of God's permanence and power as Creator of everything. Starting with God's promise and instructions to go where he would be shown, he had now internalized that promise— "I [Jehovah] will bless those who bless you [Abram]"—to the point of the actions at Beersheba. He was about to receive another instruction to go where "I will tell you"[117] that would test and expand the relationship at the highest level.

117. Gen. 22:2.

At the Peak

Genesis 22

Now these things happened to them as an example, and they were
written for our instruction.

1 CORINTHIANS 10:11

CYCLE 16 IS A test. It is a test that comes "after these things" (Gen. 22:1). It
is a test of Abraham's heart, but only after preparation and training. Abram
had been called from Haran thirty-eight years before.[1] He had received
promises, cut a covenant, had his name changed, and was circumcised. He
had seen God's hand of protection and His hand of judgment. In his old
age, he had received from God a son. Having blessed Abraham abundantly,
God wanted to know his heart, or, more accurately, God wanted the reader
to know Abraham's heart.

Importantly, the reader is told it is a test immediately so no misunderstanding can occur,[2] specifically to avoid NO HOPE in the reader. The
word in verse 1 of Genesis 22 is *nacah:* to test, to prove. In the King James
rendition, it also means to tempt. In 1611, when the King James Version
was translated, the English word "tempt" meant to prove or test. Over time
the meaning of tempt has changed, much as "terrific" no longer means ter-
rifying. In game theory today, "incredible" still has the negative meaning
"not credible," much different from its extremely positive common use.

---

1. Possibly as long as sixty-two years.

2. Kass, *The Beginning of Wisdom,* 334.

71

Abraham did not know it was a proving, of course. If he had known it was only a test, it would have been no test at all. The reader is in a position of needing to understand Abraham's emotions and thoughts without personally feeling the uncertainty of Mt. Moriah. The tradeoff is necessary because most readers have children or loved ones who make empathizing with Abraham in the Mt. Moriah situation quite easy, but they have no good way of understanding the patriarch's attack on four armies with only 318 men or receiving the long-promised first-born at age one hundred. Without Abraham's full experience, it would be easy to come away from this story feeling bitter toward God. To help us learn Moriah's lessons, we are told on the front end that it was a test.

"Take now your son, your only son"—there would be no possible fallback onto Ishmael— "whom you love, Isaac." Twenty-two chapters into the Bible, this is the first use of the word love. "[A]nd go to the land (*eretz*) of Moriah." Moriah means "a place of God's choosing." God chose the man, the time, and the place. "[O]ffer him there as a burnt offering on one of the mountains[3] which I will tell you." The burnt offering left nothing; it was an offering of total dedication. The Hebrew is *ola*, meaning "to go up" and signifying both the offering going up in smoke and the relationship of the one bringing the offering toward Jehovah ascending as if going up stairs.[4] If we consider our perspective of Abraham's perspective, there appears to be NO HOPE, but here is where we go wrong if we fail to consider Abraham's changing relationship with Jehovah. Indeed, Abraham's understanding is quite different: "He considered that God is able to raise people even from the dead, from which he also received him back as a type."[5] Abraham had *caphar*-ed the stars and believed Jehovah.

"So Abraham rose early in the morning." Abraham never had trouble making decisions: when the famine struck, he went to Egypt; when the grass ran out, he parted with his nephew, Lot; "when Abram heard that

---

3. Historically this is said to be the site of the temple in Jerusalem. As this information would be an exciting and important part of Jewish history, the specific site should have been preserved. 2 Sam. 24:18: So Gad came to David that day and said to him, "Go up, erect an altar to the LORD on the threshing floor of Araunah the Jebusite."

2 Chron. 3:1: "Then Solomon began to build the house of the LORD in Jerusalem on Mount Moriah, where the LORD had appeared to his father David, at the place that David had prepared on the threshing floor of Ornan the Jebusite." Four hundred years in Egypt might have blurred things, however.

4. *Strong's* H5930.

5. Heb. 11:19.

his relative had been taken captive, he led out his trained men"[6]; when he caught up with Chedorlaomer, he attacked; when God laid out the covenant of circumcision, he circumcised every male in his house "the very same day."[7] After God told him to honor Sarah's wishes, he rose early in the morning to send Hagar and his son Ishmael away.

"[H]e split the wood for the burnt offering"[8] and on arriving at Mt. Moriah he left the young men with the donkey. The young men he took with him would have nothing to do with Isaac's death.

What Abraham did not do was protest. He *had* protested in past cycles. When God promised a great reward, Abraham protested that he had no heir.[9] He asked for a sign that he would receive the land.[10] He questioned God about sweeping away the wicked with the righteous in Sodom.[11] But when he was told to sacrifice Isaac as a burnt offering, he saddled his donkey and headed for Moriah. For three days he considered Isaac as good as dead but was preparing to receive him back by a miracle of God.

As tempting as it is to see Isaac as a type of Christ carrying the wood for his death up the mountain, there are limitations. First, it was a test. Second, Genesis 22:2 makes it clear this was a burnt offering, not a sin offering. Nevertheless, it is difficult not to notice the similarities.

"On the third day Abraham raised his eyes and saw the place from a distance."[12] He had had three nights and three days to think. Helpfully, we are told in Hebrews 11:19 that "he considered that God was able to raise men even from the dead." "Considered" means "to occupy oneself with calculations." He was probably occupied at night looking at the stars and reviewing the story of redemption. He might have thought about the genealogy of Genesis 5[13] (an oral tradition for Abraham) that confirmed the message of the stars. He was occupied during the day remembering the promises of his descendants becoming a great nation, of them blessing the whole earth, and of recalling that "in Isaac your descendants shall be

6. Gen. 14:14
7. Gen. 17:23.
8. Gen. 22:3.
9. Gen. 15:2.
10. Gen. 15:8.
11. Gen. 18:23.
12. Gen. 22:4.
13. See Appendix C.

called."[14] Undoubtedly, he thought back to when he received the amazing promise of a son "from his own body" at an advanced age:

> . . . and without becoming weak in faith he contemplated his own body, now as good as dead since he was about a hundred years old, and the deadness of Sarah's womb; yet, with respect to the promise of God, he did not waver in unbelief, but grew strong in faith, giving glory to God, and being fully assured that what He had promised, He was able to perform. [15]

Abraham must have particularly remembered the conversation after Jehovah laid out His covenant and its sign of circumcision: "Sarah your wife shall bear you a son, and you shall call his name Isaac, and I will establish My covenant with him for an everlasting covenant for his descendants after him."[16]

Considering that he was to offer Isaac as a burnt offering, he received strength knowing Jehovah as Creator of heaven and earth "who gives life to the dead and calls into being that which does not exist,"[17] and "by faith we understand that the worlds were prepared by the word of God, so that what is seen was not made out of things which are visible."[18] The words are from the New Testament; Abraham's understanding and his faith were from God.

Here as elsewhere, Abraham had a conversation(s) with God of which we are not told details. Initially (Gen. 22:2) God had instructed him to offer Isaac "on one of the mountains which I will tell you." By verse 9, "they came to the place of which God had told him." When the more specific instructions came, Abraham might have had questions.

Whatever was said between the two of them, Abraham had not yet told Isaac what God had told him. The two left the young men and the donkey, laying the wood on Isaac.

As they climbed up together, Abraham explained what God had told him to do. Abraham was at least 113 years old and "as good as dead."[19] Isaac was probably thirteen (the age of Ishmael when Isaac was born; Isaac was still called a "lad," but he was old enough to carry the wood. He could have

---

14. Heb. 11:18 quoting Gen. 21:12.

15. Rom. 4:19–21.

16. Gen. 17:19.

17. Rom. 4:17.

18. Heb. 11:3.

19. Rom. 4:19, Heb. 11:12.

been as old as thirty-six). Isaac could have successfully resisted, but God had chosen Abraham "in order that he may command his children and his household after him to keep the way of the Lord by doing righteousness and justice."[20] As Abraham obeyed God, so Isaac obeyed Abraham.

As father and son started up the mountain (22:7), Isaac did not know God's instructions about the offering: "Where is the lamb?" he asked. By their arrival (v. 9) Abraham had explained to Isaac what they were to do, another off-stage conversation, but a synthesis of Abraham's three days of calculations. Isaac arrived with a fuller understanding of his father's heart for God and had accepted his place in God's promises and plans.

Abraham raised the knife to make the sacrifice, BUT GOD called from heaven. Several things had changed. First, although Elohim set up the test (22:1), the angel of the Lord stopped it. "Angel" comes into focus in verse 12: "*now I know* that you fear God, since you have not withheld your son, your only son, from *Me*" (emphasis mine). Next, the offering changed from the lamb of the guilt offering Abraham and Isaac had discussed while walking up the mountain, to the ram[21] of the burnt offering,[22] the offering of total dedication. Then, in an ACT OF LOVE, God revealed himself as Jehovah Jireh, and in an ACT OF FAITH Abraham changed the name of that place to "The Lord Will Provide."[23]

As Jehovah Jireh leads His people into new areas (places or understanding)—off the ark, out of Egypt, up Moriah, from the grave—He provides safe harbor, manna, a ram, new life.

Genesis One	Genesis 2–11	Genesis 12–21
Light (Kingdom)	Eden	Abram
Vertical Separation (Water)	Fall	Egypt
Horizontal Separation	Cain Kills Able	Lot
Seeds	Genesis 5 Genealogy	Promise of Seed
Signs (Sun and Moon)	Rainbow	Circumcision
Birds	Dove with Olive Branch	Moriah
Man	Family	Tribe

For expanded chart see Appendix E.

20. Gen. 18:19.
21. Gen. 22:13.
22. Lev. 1:10.
23. Gen. 22:14.

The angel of the Lord called again. Until the second call, Abraham had been dealing with God through promises (conditional: you do this, and I will respond in a positive way) and covenants (penalties imposed for non-compliance). Now God interposed with an oath, "By myself I have sworn."[24] The oath was not required. God added it to demonstrate His pleasure with Abraham:

> For when God made the promise to Abraham, since He could swear by no one greater, He swore by Himself . . . For men swear by one greater than themselves, and with them an oath given as confirmation is an end of every dispute. In the same way God, desiring even more to show to the heirs of the promise the unchangeableness of His purpose, interposed with an oath, in order that by two unchangeable things, in which it is impossible for God to lie, we may have strong encouragement, we who have fled for refuge in laying hold of the hope set before us. [25]

Abraham had met the conditions; the promises were his: ". . . because you have done this thing, and have not withheld your son, your only son, I will greatly bless you" (v. 16). "[B]ecause you have obeyed My voice all the nations of *eretz* shall be blessed" (v. 18). The condition was obedience; obedience requires faith; faith is giving God His due, which is why Abraham went up the mountain. "I and the lad will go yonder; and we will worship and return to you."[26] Worship means "to bow down to a superior." Many years later God extended the covenant to Isaac "because Abraham obeyed Me and kept My charge, My commandments, My statutes and My laws."[27]

The promise was changed slightly. Abraham left Haran with a promise that "in you all the families of *adamah* shall be blessed,"[28] a promise that was now extended to *eretz*. Also added was the phrase "your seed shall possess the gate of their enemies." [29]

We see Abraham's act of obedience corresponding with this oft-quoted passage: "For God so loved the world that He gave His only begotten Son,

24. Gen. 22:16.

25. Heb. 6:13–18.

26. Gen. 22:5.

27. Gen. 26:5.

28. Gen. 12:3.

29. Gen. 22:17 "Seed" is singular in verses 17 and 18. In Gal. 3:16, Paul points to the word seed: "Now the promises were spoken to Abraham and to his seed. He does not say, 'And to seeds,' as referring to many, but rather to one, 'And to your seed,' that is, Christ."

that whoever believes in Him shall not perish, but have eternal life."[30] For Abraham so loved God, that he gave his only begotten son and became the father of faith, a powerful demonstration of the truth that whoever believes in God's Christ shall not perish but have everlasting life.

Genesis 22:19 states that "Abraham returned to his young men, and they arose and went together to Beersheba." There is no mention of Isaac returning. Possibly he stayed on Moriah with God. He too had demonstrated faith. He needed time alone with the God whom heretofore he had known only as his father's God but who now had become his own. (Jacob would refer to Jehovah as "the Fear of Isaac.")[31]

Isaac would find his place in the Hebrews' Hall of Faith chapter, namely 11:20: "By faith Isaac blessed Jacob and Esau, even regarding things to come." He would also join a very exclusive group—he walked with God.[32]

Abraham had four major events in his growth with Jehovah; he received a call, a covenant, a son, and that son back from the dead.

In His most laudatory and touching testimony of Abraham's faith, God calls him "Abraham, my friend."[33] Abraham left Haran not knowing where he was going, with only a promise and the name of God. He left Moriah having arrived where he was sent, the friend of Jehovah. Perhaps Oswald Chambers had Abraham in mind when he penned these eloquent words: "One life wholly devoted to God is of more value to God than one hundred lives simply awakened by His Spirit."[34]

---

30. John 3:16.

31. Gen. 21:42.

32. Gen. 48:15.

33. Isa. 41:8

34. Chambers, *My Utmost for His Highest*, April 24.

And Some Other Things Happened

Genesis 23–50

Now these things happened to them as an example,
and they were written for our instruction.

1 CORINTHIANS 10:11

THE CYCLES WE HAVE been following continue to the end of Genesis (see Appendix D). Joseph's story is a journey with Jehovah, much like Abraham's, and deserves some examination, at least on that one level.

The Genesis story is heavily intertwined—we have seen similarities between the creation and the flood narratives, Adam and Abram, and instances of certain words being used in only two or three stories, which draw them together, such as "desire" and "rule" in chapters 3 and 4. These are the only uses of *tesuqa*, desire (Eve for Adam and sin for Cain), in the Pentateuch; *masal*, rule (Adam over Eve and Cain over sin), is used in both sentences.[1]

Genesis is also intertwined with the rest of the Pentateuch—think Abram going to Egypt in a famine and the exodus story. Our theme is the cycles of Genesis, one that does not lend itself well to much exploration of these important comparisons. I will address some of the themes in Section 3.

The story in the Pentateuch rises to its second peak in Genesis 22 on Moriah.[2] This is the pinnacle of faith, the ultimate type: Abraham offered

1. This was discussed more fully in cycle 3.
2. The first was creation, the next will be the exodus.

his "only begotten son" as a burnt offering solely because Jehovah required it. Whereas Moses is a type of Christ—leading the sheep, giving the law, interceding by standing between God and a disobedient Israel, etc., Abraham is a type of God the Father, acting as God would act, believing what God believes, and having a relationship with the promised son as Jehovah would have with His Christ during His earthly ministry.

Faith is defined by Abraham. The remainder of the Pentateuch is How to Live 101. Israel rebels, things go bad, God intervenes, Israel moves on—the pattern of Genesis written on a national scale.

Cycle 17, three chapters starting in Genesis 23, is the story of Isaac post-Moriah. Isaac is the only Genesis character born in the Promised Land who did not leave at some point. This may be the direct effect of something Jehovah had impressed upon his father back in cycle 8. The night that God showed Abram the stars, Abram had implored Him to explain how he would know that he would inherit the land. Jehovah responded, "Know for certain that your descendants will be strangers in a land that is not theirs, where they will be enslaved and oppressed for four hundred years."[3] One way to avoid enslavement in a foreign land is to not leave home.

Another result of that conversation, which included a warning about the iniquity of the Amorites among whom they lived and had alliances, was an oath regarding Isaac that Abram made his servant swear, saying that when Isaac came of age, "by the LORD, the God of heaven and the God of earth, that you shall not take a wife for my son from the daughters of the Canaanites, among whom I live but you will go to my country and to my relatives, and take a wife for my son Isaac."[4] Abraham further added the command, "Beware that you do not take my son back [to Haran]."[5]

Because a wife from Egypt seemed out of the question given Abram's personal experience with Pharaoh and the Hagar disaster, this set up an interesting family dynamic when it came to wives and life-and-death travel plans. Isaac did not leave home, and the servant brought Rebekah from Haran.

Allow a quick digression to link these events to those of cycles 18, 19, and 21. When Esau planned to kill Jacob for stealing his blessing and birthright, Isaac and Rebekah, surely aware of the "know for certain"

3. Gen. 15:8 and 13.
4. Gen. 24:3 and 4.
5. Gen. 24:6.

four-hundred-year enslavement problem hanging in the air, had a tough choice since Jacob had to leave town. Egypt still was stigmatized and hiding out among the Amorites would be foolish given that the enslavement was to avoid Amorite iniquity, leaving Haran as the only escape destination. Abraham and Rebekah were both from there, and he had forbidden his son to return. She had little choice. Haran was a risk, but it wasn't Ur of the Chaldeans.

Things went well at first, but soon Jacob was tricked and undoubtedly felt enslaved in a foreign land. He fled, was pursued, and God intervened.

Years later, when Jacob, now renamed Israel, was in another life-and-death situation (drought), Haran was the stigmatized choice, and he sent his sons to Egypt for relief. God had used Joseph to prepare the way for the whole clan to move south. Again, everything went well at first, but eventually they were enslaved, fled/were driven out, were pursued, and God intervened. From God's view, at least, Egypt was not going to be easy, but it wasn't the land of the Amorites.

Now back to cycle 17. Isaac's mother died, his half-brother had been sent away, and his wife was barren. He had was NO HOPE. BUT GOD blessed Isaac and opened Rebekah's womb.[6] When Rebekah sought the Lord about the pregnancy, in a WORD OF LOVE He told her that "Two nations are in your womb; and two peoples will be separated from your body; and one people shall be stronger than the other; and the older shall serve the younger."[7] This prophesy probably affected Rebekah's actions regarding the two boys years later, as we shall see in Section 3. Reading on, we find a FAITH-BUILD-ING event where God appeared to Isaac and extended the covenant He had made with Abraham to him.

Now we examine the making of Israel.

Isaac had two sons, Jacob and Esau. Their story is found in Genesis 28–34 in cycles 18, 19, and 20. They were twins, even harder to tell apart than the sons of faith and bondage in cycle 14. Esau was a man of the field, an accomplished hunter, an outdoorsman, a man's man. Jacob, living in tents, was a peaceful man and his mother's favorite.[8] Their hearts were different. Esau grew to despise his birthright. Jacob, staying near home, was closer to the people who knew God. For the first twelve years or so, that

6. Gen. 25:11 and 21.

7. Gen. 25:23.

8. Gen. 25:27 and 28.

included his grandfather, Abraham, who no doubt told him the stories of leaving Ur, the adventures and misadventures in Egypt with Pharaoh, his battles with northern kings, but mostly his discussions with God. They talked about promises and covenants, how to caphar stars all night, and what it was like to fight off birds of prey all day. He got to hear about Mt. Moriah from the perspectives of both the father and the son. Jacob desired the birthright that Esau despised.

Nothing is the matter with being a great hunter. Nimrod was a mighty hunter before the Lord.[9] Esau's understanding of himself was not who he was in God, but who he was in the field. There is inherent good in the path Jacob chose (or was chosen for him). Jacob was not without skills of the field. He was quite a herdsman and skillful breeder, as Laban would learn. He was a "peaceful" man.[10] The Hebrew is *tam,* meaning complete, whole, or upright. It is derived from *taman,* a word used nine times to describe Job. When God said, "Jacob I loved, but Esau I hated,"[11] it was a judgment of their hearts. While Esau was in the field, Jacob was in the tents learning from Abraham, who, when put to the ultimate test, answered as God's Christ would: "Not my will but Yours be done." Jacob learned that lesson; Esau was not around.

Likewise, I can leave the tents and seek my fortune in the fields. I can despise my birthright. This is easier than it sounds. I can find a great treasure in a field and give everything I have to own that field and get the treasure. Then one day I look around the field and notice the fence needs repair, then the gate, and soon discover that the creekbank is eroding. Furthermore, I can subdivide the field and sell lots. I can become so wealthy or so occupied that the original treasure of the field is forgotten. I started with the heart of Jacob, became Esau, and never noticed.

It is always a heart thing with God. My heart is where I place my trust. *In what* do I have faith? If I am not sure or I am not paying attention to my decisions, I will follow my money.[12]

We will examine the deception of Isaac in Section 3.

Cycle 18 begins in Genesis 27:41 with Esau vowing to kill his brother for the wrongs Jacob has done him. Both Rebekah and Isaac recognize

---

9. Gen. 10:9.

10. Gen. 25:27.

11. Rom. 9:13 and Mal. 1:3.

12. Matt. 6:21: "for where your treasure is, there your heart will be also."

Jacob's life is in real danger, and neither is in a position to stop Esau—they had NO HOPE. Isaac did the only thing he could by sending Jacob to the relatives, BUT GOD met Jacob in a dream his first night on the road. In an ACT OF LOVE, He extended the promise of Abraham and Isaac to Jacob: "Behold, I am with you and will keep you wherever you go, and will bring you back to this land; for I will not leave you until I have done what I have promised you."[13]

Jacob responds with a vow of his own. Like his father on Moriah and his grandfather leaving Haran not knowing where he was going, Jacob started BUILDING FAITH in a direct relationship with Jehovah: "If God will be with me and will keep me on this journey that I take, and will give me food to eat and garments to wear, and I return to my father's house in safety, then the Lord will be my God. This stone, which I have set up as a pillar, will be God's house, and of all that You give me I will surely give a tenth to You."[14]

In **cycle 19** it is déjà vu all over again for Jacob. Earlier he had taken advantage of his father's inability to see, and thus gained a blessing; in this cycle Laban takes advantage of Jacob's inability to see (night, bridal veil, wine, and probably more wine) and marries off an older daughter. Circumstances deteriorate from there, and in Genesis 31:1 things change from Jacob's resenting his father-in-law to fearing him. A dangerous Laban if he stays, a dangerous Esau if he goes, there was NO HOPE. BUT GOD meets him in his need, and in Genesis 31:13 we read God's instructions to him regarding how to deal with the quandary: "I am the God of Bethel, where you anointed a pillar, where you made a vow to Me; now arise, leave this land, and return to the land of your birth."

The trickster had no easy road. First there are the logistics of moving a large family and larger herds, which he tried to do without Laban finding out. Then, when that failed, he had to deal with an irritated Laban—and on

---

13. Gen. 28:15 offers a point of interest: Although God says He is the God of Isaac (v. 13) and Jehovah told Abraham that He would extend the covenant to Isaac, there is no place that describes the actual extension of Abraham's covenant (land, descendants, blessing to earth) to Isaac, as is being extended to Jacob in this passage. Indeed, Ps. 105:9 speaks of "the covenant which He made with Abraham, And *His oath* to Isaac" (emphasis mine).

14. Gen. 28:20–22 gives a second point of interest from the story: this is the first "house of God" in Scripture. Many more, including the two temples in Jerusalem, would follow.

top of everything else, Rachel had stolen her father's idol! Then Jacob learns Esau is coming with four hundred armed men. "Four hundred" is one of those terms meaning "enough to do the job." In Esau's defense, Jacob was coming toward him with a large force as well, and their prior dealings had been confrontational.

Jacob had a lot of balls in the air and was not sleeping well. Sending everyone ahead in groups, he stayed back to think. In an all-night wrestling match that at first is hard to see as an ACT OF LOVE, God met him in his moment of distress. God dislocated Jacob's hip and changed his name to Israel.[15] Jacob was ecstatic. "So Jacob named the place Peniel, for he said, 'I have seen God face to face, yet my life has been preserved.'"[16]

In the Hall of Faith chapter, Hebrews 11, Jacob is listed with the other men of faith and described as "leaning on his staff," a direct result of his wrestle and dislocation. It is not even clear, short of that FAITH-BUILDING experience, that Jacob would have crossed Peniel to face his brother. (He had sent them in groups so that some could escape if Esau's motives proved nasty. He in effect was the last and smallest group, most capable of escape if he waited for events to unfold.)

In **cycle** 20 Jacob/Israel has a new fear. His sons had slaughtered a whole town to avenge their sister's rape. He stated his situation succinctly: "You have brought trouble on me by making me odious among the inhabitants of the land, among the Canaanites and the Perizzites; and my men being few in number, they will gather together against me and attack me and I will be destroyed, I and my household."[17]

He had NO HOPE.

BUT GOD appeared to Jacob and gave him new instructions. He moved to Bethel, where he always ended up in times of distress, which were many for someone who "strives with men and with God." He also put away any foreign gods kept by those of his household, changed garments, and built yet another altar.[18] In an ACT OF LOVE God appeared to him and blessed him: "I am God Almighty; Be fruitful and multiply; A nation and a multitude of nations shall come from you, And kings shall come forth from you."[19]

15. Gen. 32:25.
16. Gen. 32:30.
17. Gen. 34:30.
18. Gen. 35:2–3.
19. Gen. 35:10–12.

To BUILD FAITH God promised him (most of) the land promised to Abraham and Isaac.[20]

The least to be learned from these three cycles is that Jacob, the supplanter,[21] who strove with God and men and even though he prevailed,[22] at the end of his life "Jacob said to Pharaoh, 'The years of my sojourning are one hundred and thirty; few and unpleasant have been the years of my life, nor have they attained the years that my fathers lived during the days of their sojourning.'"[23]

In our retrospective view, it is hard to see that all the striving, conniving, wrestling, and tricks got Jacob anything but his name changed to Israel.[24] True, he got Esau's birthright and blessing, but Esau's heart was indifferent to the promise and to Isaac, Abraham, and even to Jehovah. He probably would have given everything up anyway. Even Jacob's name change to Israel means "God prevails,"[25] not Jacob prevails.

Jacob could not see, as we can, the pattern of God moving the younger ahead of the older: Seth, Isaac, Jacob, Ephraim, Kings Saul and David, the Christian church (versus the Jewish nation). We can easily imagine a scenario whereby the result would be the same with a lot less hassle if Jacob had applied Abraham's faith and trust, but that is the lesson of these cycles and the very reason they are cycles. We all have our own cycles and opportunities to apply Abraham's faith and patience.

With faith and patience in mind, let us turn our attention briefly to the remainder of Genesis, **cycle 21**. I have chosen to incorporate chapters 37–50 into the one cycle for reasons that will soon be seen. Joseph was stripped of his identity, thrown into a pit, and would be killed by his own brothers. He had NO HOPE. BUT GOD "was with Joseph" repeatedly. In fact, this cycle has four sub-cycles: slavery and favor with Potiphar; trouble with Mrs. Potiphar and favor with the jailor; being forgotten by the cupbearer and favor with Pharaoh; and the Judah/Tamar dust-up which changed Judah's life.

---

20. Ishmael got some from Abram, Esau got some from Isaac.

21. Hebrew *ya aqob, Strong's* H3290: supplanter.

22. Gen. 32:28.

23. Gen. 47:9.

24. Gen. 32:28.

25. Hebrew *Yisra'el, Strong's* H3478

In an ACT OF LOVE Jacob adopted Joseph's Egyptian-born sons, and to BUILD Joseph's FAITH he gave those sons a blessing/prophesy that further united them with the family and heritage. Build faith it did indeed, as years later, despite a situation in Egypt that looked very advantageous, Joseph would be able to see the exodus back to the land that God had promised his forefathers.

Joseph's story is a journey into hope, and the easiest way for me to portray his life *in toto* is to graph it using a "happiness scale" from one to ten, one being lowest of lows and ten being the best, to assess where he is at points in the Genesis narrative. Time is on the X axis, but to no standard scale.

More because of the mother than the son, Joseph was his father's favorite. What is worse, Joseph was not bashful about this partiality. He was given a coat of many colors displaying his favored status and he wore it—not just at festivals or family gatherings; he wore it all the time. That was not the best idea for someone with ten older brothers. At the start of chapter 37, from Joseph's seventeen-year-old point of view, all was good. I would rate his happiness as an eight (he had to be aware of his brother's animosity to some degree, since "they hated him and could not speak to him on friendly terms" (v. 4).

When a story starts at a height, it likely will have a fall. Jacob sent Joseph to Shechem to see about his brothers' welfare, but they had moved their camp. Joseph caught them at Dothan, but they saw him coming, and, remembering how he had previously given their father a bad report about them, plotted to kill him.

They threw Joseph into a well and went back to their camp to eat. Note: campsites are chosen to be near water, so it was probably at some distance, since the well they threw Joseph into was dry. While they were eating, "some Midianite traders passed by, so they [the Midianites] pulled him up and lifted Joseph out of the pit, and sold him to the Ishmaelites,"[26] who sold him into Egyptian slavery. I give that a two instead of a one only because some of his brothers would have killed him if God had not sent the Midianites and the Ishmaelite caravan to the right place at the right time.

---

26. Gen. 37:28. There is ancient debate on whether the Midianites were ruled by Ishmaelites and thus considered Ishmaelites themselves, in which case Joseph's brothers would have pulled him out and sold him.

The Ramban[27] points out that years later, in Genesis 42:21, as the brothers stood before a hostile Egyptian viceroy whom they did not recognize as Joseph, they lamented their treatment of brother Joseph. Specifically, not that they had sold him into slavery, the worse crime, but that "we saw the distress of his soul when he pleaded with us {from the pit], yet we would not listen." That is, throwing him into the pit against his pleas for mercy was as far as they got. That is why Reuben was surprised when he came to rescue his brother that Joseph was not still in the pit.[28]

Things could have been worse in Egypt. Joseph lands in Potiphar's house and prospers—not favored-son status, but not a pit. I give this a six by virtue of his relief from facing a worse fate, but Potiphar's wife changed that. Joseph is thrown into a serious Egyptian prison. He has NO reason for HOPE; that must be a one on our scale.

BUT GOD gave him favor with the jailer, so his situation crept up and advanced further when one of the men whose dreams he (correctly) interpreted was restored to a favored position at Pharaoh's court. Joseph had admonished the cupbearer to "Only keep me in mind when it goes well with you, and please do me a kindness by mentioning me to Pharaoh and get me out of this house."[29] His hopes no doubt soared. Compared to his first day in jail, watching the cupbearer being redeemed was a nine. Then, a cruel letdown: "Yet the chief cupbearer did not remember Joseph, but forgot him,"[30] and "two full years" passed. Down to three (he still had favor with the jailer).

Then Pharaoh had his dreams, and the cupbearer finally remembered Joseph. Pharaoh consulted him, was happy with the interpretation, and elevated him to the number two man in all of Egypt. That must have felt good, but with a young life now filled with ups and downs (and remembering the baker), his "happiness" was probably tempered to a seven or eight, say seven-and-a-half. (A famine was still coming that he had to deal with.)

The famine was expected; the brothers were not. What should Joseph do? How should he react? After all, they had stripped off his two coats—the coat that signified he was one of Jacob's sons and the multicolored coat that

---

27. The RaMbaN (1194-1270), also known as Nachmanides, was a Spanish Talmudist who is often referenced regarding Torah interpretation. I am presenting his understanding of the sale of Joseph.

28. Gen. 37:30. Sefaria, *the RaMBaN on Genesis*.

29. Gen. 40:14.

30. Gen. 40:23.

signified he was Jacob's favorite among them. In doing so, they in effect disowned him—those of the brothers that did not want him dead. But they were his brothers, and all had come out fairly well. Still there was the matter of the two dreams he'd had back in Canaan, with his brothers bowing down and such. So, he decided on the family tradition passed down from Abraham to Isaac ("this woman is my sister") to Jacob ("I am Esau") to these very brothers (implying that Joseph was killed by wild beasts)—the ruse. He just played himself, Egyptian Numero Dos, and left out the "I'm your brother" part.

This had mixed results. His father eventually let Benjamin go down to Egypt, and Joseph might have gotten Jacob to come to Egypt eventually inside of the ruse, but he could not pull it off, broke down, and revealed himself to his brothers. Carts were sent to pick up his father. When everyone got settled in Goshen, Joseph was happy indeed. At least a nine, probably a ten when Jacob got there.

There was a bit of a downer following Jacob's death when it came out that his treacherous brothers suspected that Joseph might be planning some treachery of his own, but that was worked out. Still, coupled with his father's death, it spoiled the mood. Down to eight.

A plot of the events looks like this:

Joseph's life

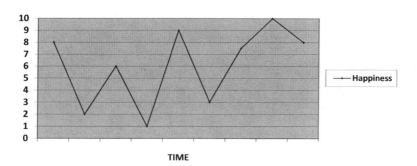

TIME

Two parts of the story command our attention. First, Joseph had two dreams.[31] He would tell Pharaoh that the second dream "means that the matter is determined by God, and God will *quickly* bring it about" (emphasis

31. Gen. 37:6 and 9.

87

mine).[32] He went to Egypt at age seventeen and stood before Pharaoh "when he was thirty years old."[33] Thirteen years is a slow "quickly" for most of us, but Joseph looked Pharaoh in the eye and told him he needed to move fast. That is an indication of God working in his heart, as we shall see.

The second part worthy of noting, but as a side drama, is the Judah-Tamar story in Genesis 38. Judah goes from the brother who wanted to sell Joseph into slavery[34] to the brother who was entrusted to take Benjamin to Egypt.[35] God had used Tamar to show Judah his own heart and to effect change. More on this in Section 3.

Also interesting is Reuben's failure to change. As the oldest, he was the one who should have been the leader of his brothers, but he disgraced himself when he "lay with Bilhah his father's concubine."[36] Jacob did not trust him to take Benjamin to Egypt, no doubt because he had not seen the heart change in Reuben that he had seen in Judah, but also because of Reuben's rationale for trusting him: "You may put my two sons to death if I do not bring [Benjamin] back to you; put him in my care, and I will return him to you."[37] In effect his guarantee was, "if I cause you to lose your son, you can kill your grandsons."

Now let us look at the same story, but instead of Joseph's happiness rating, let's consider his heart attitudes, particularly toward Jehovah. To do that we have to go by his own words as our sole guide—we will try to discern how much he is thinking of Jehovah versus only himself. We will take his words and rank them on the same zero to ten scale with zero being no God/all Joseph and ten being all God.

We start in Genesis 37 when Joseph is proudly telling the family about his dreams. "He said to them, 'Please listen to this dream which I have had,'"[38] then, "Lo, I have had still another dream; and behold, the sun and the moon and eleven stars were bowing down to me."[39] That is all Joseph. "I" had the dream. "I" stand up and you bow down. No mention of God

32. Gen. 41:32.
33. Gen. 42:46.
34. Gen. 37:26.
35. Gen. 43:3–14.
36. Gen. 35:22.
37. Gen. 42:37.
38. Gen. 37:6.
39. Gen. 37:9.

giving the dreams or interpreting them. God zero and Joseph ten; in other words, a 0/10 is a zero rating on the chart.

Next, we pick him up dealing with Mrs. Potiphar. "There is no one greater in this house than I, and [Potiphar] has withheld nothing from me except you, because you are his wife. How then could I do this great evil and sin against God?"[40] That is still a lot of I, but God gets a significant mention. God three, Joseph seven.

When he is in the dungeon with the baker and cupbearer and told they each had dreams, he replies, "Do not interpretations belong to God? Tell it to me, please."[41] God gets first mention, but Joseph is a valuable partner. Five all.

Standing before Pharaoh—who wants to be thought of as a god—after all the court magicians have failed to interpret his dream, and possibly with his head on the line, "Joseph then answered Pharaoh, saying, 'It is not in me; God will give Pharaoh a favorable answer.'"[42] Some God, some me, but God gets a mention at a time when implying there is a God higher than Pharaoh or his gods might not work out so well. God six, Joseph four.

Next, Joseph is standing before his brothers, having just identified himself as the brother they sold into slavery. "Now do not be grieved or angry with yourselves, because you sold me here, for God sent me before you to preserve life." Clearly, he is thinking about someone besides himself. He empathizes with their emotions and fears, and lends comfort. He places God as in control of all events, implying he will remain in control. God eight, Joseph two.

After Israel died, the brothers thought Joseph might have been waiting for that moment to exact revenge. They came and fell down before him, but he answered, "Do not be afraid, for am I in God's place? As for you, you meant evil against me, but God meant it for good in order to bring about this present result, to preserve many people alive."[43] Doubtless God had used Joseph's time as a slave and a prisoner, and also his time as CEO of Egypt, to change his heart. God nine, Joseph one.

Finally, as he was dying, "Joseph made the sons of Israel swear, saying, 'God will surely take care of you, and you shall carry my bones up from here.'"[44] This is all God; it is prophesy. It has no Joseph because it will

40. Gen. 39:9.
41. Gen. 40:8.
42. Gen. 41:16.
43. Gen. 50:19–20.
44. Gen. 50:25.

come about years after he is dead. Joseph has taken his place among the patriarchs.

Adding the heart to the happiness graph:

Joseph, A Life

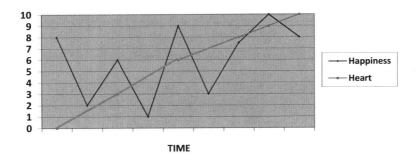

I can guarantee your happiness graph will look something like Joseph's, up and down. How your heart graph looks is up to you.

Cycle 21 could be divided into a number of sub-cycles, but as it is one narrative, I will keep it together. After his brothers disowned him and he was sold into slavery, he had NO HOPE, BUT GOD gave him favor with Potiphar, the jailor, and then Pharaoh. God's LOVING PROVISION became apparent during the coming famine, and the BUILDING OF FAITH is apparent in Joseph's life, culminating in his vision that reached beyond his family's position when they were well provided for in Goshen, to see God's promise that they would be given Canaan.

Joseph's last words to his brothers were, "I am about to die, but God will surely take care of you and bring you up from this land to the land which He promised on oath to Abraham, to Isaac and to Jacob."[45]

We have seen a series of situations with NO HOPE. They were not going to get better on their own, even if given time. BUT GOD intervened. He redeemed the situation; He took a situation that was formless and void, and added light; in a sense He atoned for the situation. If we see each cycle as a mini-atonement, we are preparing ourselves for *the* Atonement.

Oswald Chambers captures this idea with clarity: "The Atonement of Jesus has to work out in practical, unobtrusive ways in my life. Every time

45. Gen. 50:24.

I obey, absolute Deity is on my side, so that the grace of God and natural obedience coincide. Obedience means that I have banked everything on the Atonement, and my obedience is met immediately by the delight of the supernatural grace of God."[46]

---

46. Chambers, *My Utmost for His Highest*, October 9.

Searching the Scriptures

Search the Scriptures! You think that in them you have eternal life; it
is these that testify about Me.

JOHN 5:39[1]

As WE HAVE SEEN in each of the cycles, when the next crisis develops, God responds to redeem the situation. We have focused on *what* God's intervention was and *how* it affected the protagonists of the stories. Let's now take a brief look at the *who* of these interventions. Can we infer anything about the who of these interactions from the protagonists' point of view?

In cycle one, the third Hebrew word is *Elohim,* which famously is plural for God. This is the first of many clues that suggest a Triune God. In cycle 2, as soon as Adam has a place to stand, God *formed* man (Gen. 2:7). The Hebrew means molded or squeezed into shape, implying hands. In cycle 3 God also walked in the garden, and Adam and Eve could hear Him coming, implying feet and legs. Further, they tried to hide from Him, implying that the God they talked with had a definite form and occupied definite space. Was Adam walking with Jesus in a preincarnate form similar to the post-resurrection Jesus with whom dozens of people interacted?

In cycle 5, we encounter another possible clue: "The LORD said, 'Come, let Us go down and there confuse their language.'"[2] This could be Jehovah using an imperial We, but it could also be another representation of the Triune God. In cycles 7 and 8, Abram's interaction is first with a

---

1. (NASB95 marginal note)

2. Gen 11:5 and 7

vision, then the Word of the Lord, and then someone(?) Who was inside Abram's tent and "took him outside."[3]

The angel of the Lord is the agent in cycles 9, 14, and 16. We read that Hagar "called the name of the LORD who spoke to her, 'You are a God who sees'; for she said, 'Have I even remained alive here after seeing him?'"[4] She did not seem to think she was dealing with an angel. When she was in the desert again, an angel of God called to her, then God opened her eyes.[5] The angel and God seemed to function as a team (or as one). On Mt. Moriah an angel called to Abraham, but soon changed to "you have not withheld your son, your only son, from *me*."[6]

The LORD appeared to Abram in cycle 10. The Hebrew for "appeared" means to be visible, to present oneself, or to cause to see—more than a voice. To leave he "went up" as Jesus did in his final departure from the disciples.[7] In cycles 11 and 12, three men stood opposite Abraham's tent. Two were later identified as angels, the third he called my Lord. They ate bread, meat, and milk, and then walked with Abraham as the coming events of Sodom were discussed.

In cycle 13, God dealt with Abimelech in a dream which appears to be an actual dream, and not a physical encounter.

In cycle 18—Jacob's dream about the ladder to heaven—the Lord was again *standing* either above the ladder or beside Jacob, depending on the source text. And in cycle 19, Jacob wrestled all night with a "man" who could dislocate his hip with a touch. Cycle 20 refers back to the experience at the ladder, and Jacob built an altar because God had revealed himself.

When we search the scriptures looking for Jesus, most of the cycles contain information that help us to see him.

---

3. Gen 15: 1–5
4. Gen 16:13.
5. Gen 21: 17 and 19.
6. Gen 22:12, emphasis mine
7. Luke 24:51.

Section 3

The Brothers

A distinction must always be made between the revelation of
Redemption and the conscious experience of salvation in a man's
life.

OSWALD CHAMBERS

VIEWING THE TEXT BY laying it out as a series of cycles of NO HOPE, BUT
GOD, ACT OF LOVE, and FAITH BUILDING in Section 2 does not lend itself to looking at similarities and ties between the cycles. Nothing in the
Pentateuch is standalone, so it is not possible to detail all the interactions. I
will discuss a few in this section.

Section 4 will be heavily dependent on John H. Sailhamer's textbook,
The Pentateuch as Narrative, particularly the introduction. This section
will likewise lean in large part on the work, original and organizational, of
Rabbi David Fohrman and the staff at Aleph Beta. I strongly recommend
their website, alephbeta.org, as a source of valuable insight.

Let's begin by looking at Abraham as a nation-builder. Abram was
called by God in chapter twelve, about a quarter of the way through Genesis. "I will make you a great nation," God told a seventy-five-year-old man
(v. 4) with an elderly wife only nine years his junior.[1] Ten years later,[2] still
childless and in desperation, they turned to Hagar.

---

1. When Abram was ninety-nine, Sarai was ninety, Gen. 17: 1 and 17.

2. Gen. 16:3.

95

Abram had two children, and Jehovah, who had promised nations, did not count Ishmael as an heir."[3] Isaac's wife was also infertile for a time, not conceiving until Isaac prayed for her. Rebekah had twins, the older of whom sold his birthright, married foreign women, was a constant source of irritation to his parents, and finally settled in Seir,[4] away from the family homestead and closer to his wives' families.

Finally, Jacob, after a slow start of his own,[5] had thirteen children. After three generations and several decades, the nation of Abram numbered eighteen, counting concubines. By the end of Genesis they still numbered only seventy (plus Joseph and his family). Not to worry, God got the job done while the Abram's family was in Egypt, but it might be worth a look at those early years for lessons God was writing into the family tree, especially if we remember that Adam and Eve started with just two children, neither of whom were in the line to Abram's nation. The third child, Seth, was a appointed in the stead of the murdered Abel.[6] That is only replacement-level childbearing: husband and wife producing two sons.

Here we have three sets of siblings, one from the start of humanity east of Eden, and two sets from the second re-start[7] after being called from the East back to the promised land. Despite being made up of (probably) two sets of twins, our three pairs were responsible for one murder, one threat of murder so credible that the parents advised fleeing to another country, and disrespect for the sibling so profound that it resulted in banishment. Indeed, this disagreeableness would result in a very credible death threat to Joseph, and his own banishment. Nearly sixty per cent through Genesis, we have gone from "be fruitful and multiply, and fill the earth"[8] to Jacob arriving alone back in Haran where his grandfather had started.

That is a lot of family fireworks, and not much filling the earth. We have seen this pattern before—in the beginning. As we discussed in cycle one, after the first of only six creation days God had created . . . light. The next day He separated the waters above from the waters below. A third of the way through the creation and there was still no dry land. A great

---

3. Gen. 22:2: "your only son, Isaac."

4. Gen. 32:33.

5. Leah bore his fourth child in the last verse of chapter 29.

6. Gen. 4:25: "[Eve] named him Seth, for, she said, 'God has appointed me another offspring in place of Abel.'"

7. Noah's flood was the first re-start, as discussed above.

8. Gen. 1:28.

many things happened over the next four days, which could have happened during the first two days, but, as previously discussed, God wanted our attention directed to the events of the first two days: light separated form darkness teaching us that there is a Kingdom of Light and a Kingdom of Darkness, and the firmament above separated from the firmament below demonstrating that there is a spiritual realm and a physical realm which started together and separated to make room for us. All was created in God's timing, but we ignore the lessons he is teaching through the order of events at our own peril. Therefore, I would like to give these pairs some scrutiny.

Based on the number of times we are told Adam "knew" his wife, we can assume that Cain and Abel were probably twins, but in any case, it ended badly between them. Their father was a horticulturist, but because of his sin, the ground he worked was cursed. Cain followed his father as a farmer despite (or to spite) the curse. Abel elected to avoid the curse by taking up animal husbandry. He let the animals deal with cursed ground.

If we think of the lads as types—especially if we follow clues that link the pride seen in Eve to Cain's response to God's warning that sin was crouching at the door[9] —we see Cain, the farmer, living under the curse and Abel, the shepherd, attempting to live outside of the curse.

Cain brought the first sacrifice and Abel followed, but Abel's was accepted and Cain's was not. Much literature has addressed the "why one and not the other" question, but maybe the answer is as simple as the types. Cain was defiant and embraced the curse; Abel did not. Cain threw his lot in with his parents and accepted sin and the curse; Abel sided with God and looked for a way out.

Farmers, in the development of agriculture, contributed to the growth of cities because a steady food supply allowed diversity of occupations. The farmer/shepherd tension we encounter in chapter 4 continues throughout Genesis:

- The city of Babel was judged and the inhabitants scattered across the land, many undoubtedly returning to nomadic shepherding.

- Abram was called out of the city to the life of a herdsman and tent-dweller.

- Lot failed when he went back to city life. Isaac briefly tried city living but soon returned to his tents.

9. See discussion in cycle 3 in Section 2.

- Joseph was converted by force to an urban setting, and his father, Jacob, was not sure whether Joseph's allegiance was with him or Pharaoh. When Joseph brought the rest of his family to Egypt to survive the famine, he carefully instructed them to identify themselves as shepherds.

- The children of Israel did not return to cities until those of the third generation[10] who were born in Egypt—a type for sin, slavery, and the curse — had died in the wilderness.

- God called Moses from the flocks of the desert, not from the palaces of Egypt.

- David's life proceeded in the opposite direction. David the shepherd, living on the mountainsides, wrote psalms and fought Goliath to protect God's honor; David the king, living in the city in the king's palace, was an adulterer and had Uriah murdered to protect his own honor.

- When the nation of Israel split into the northern and southern kingdoms, they were known as Joseph[11] and Judah respectively. "Joseph" was prosperous with merchants, farmers, and larger cities; "Judah" was more rural, populated with poorer shepherds. Both defied Jehovah and were overrun and exiled, but only Judah was specifically restored to the land.

The concept of blessings and curses is one of the great themes of the Pentateuch. As Israel was about to enter the Promised Land, God laid out their choice:

> See, I am setting before you today a blessing and a curse: the blessing, if you listen to the commandments of the Lord your God, which I am commanding you today; and the curse, if you do not listen to the commandments of the Lord your God, but turn aside from the way which I am commanding you today, by following other gods which you have not known (Deut. 11:26–28).

The blessing included "rain for your land in its season, the early and late rain, that you may gather in your grain and your new wine and

---

10. See Appendix B.

11. Ezekiel ("Joseph") and three minor prophets ("house of Joseph"), representing a span of nearly three hundred years, specifically refer to the northern kingdom as Joseph. See Amos 5:6, Obad. 1:18, and Zech. 10:6.

your oil,"[12] but came with the warning to "beware that your hearts are not deceived, and that you do not turn away and serve other gods and worship them."[13] Cain wanted the rain but ignored an even more specific direct warning from Jehovah that "sin is crouching at the door."[14] The result was that his curse changed from "cursed be the ground"[15] to "you are cursed from the ground."[16]

From Adam to Moses men sinned, were excluded from the Tree of Life, and died. After the law of Moses, sinners died as punishment for sin: "Christ redeemed us from the curse of the Law, having become a curse for us—for it is written, 'Cursed is everyone who hangs on a tree.'"[17] We have the same choice as Cain and Abel: live under the curse or live in Christ outside of the curse.

The second pair that bears our attention are Ishmael and Isaac. They were not twins; in fact, they had different mothers. Vastly different mothers: "For it is written that Abraham had two sons, one by the bondwoman and one by the free woman. But the son by the bondwoman was born according to the flesh, and the son by the free woman through the promise."[18] "But what does the Scripture say? 'Cast out the bondwoman and her son, for the son of the bondwoman shall not be an heir with the son of the free woman.'"[19]

Paul tells us that this is allegorically speaking, and the two women represent two covenants. We can choose which covenant to take part in.

Ishmael and Isaac also have something in common other than their father Abram. Both were named by God before they were born.[20] Ishmael was named "because the Lord has heard your affliction," and his name means "God Hears." The messenger who gave the name was speaking to Hagar in her flight from oppression. God heard her plight.

For the next decade and a half, every time Abram and Sarai heard the name, they were reminded that "God hears." In their case, what God had

12. Gen. 11:14.

13. Deut. 11:16.

14. Gen. 4:7.

15. Gen. 3:17.

16. Gen. 4:11.

17. Gal. 3:13.

18. Gal. 4:22.

19. Gal. 4:30.

20. Gen. 16:11 and Gen. 17:19..

heard was Abram's complaints to God: "O Lord GOD, what will You give me, since I am childless" and "Since You have given no offspring to me, one born in my house is my heir."[21] Their subsequent decision to use Hagar as a surrogate mother had been ill-advised and put a strain on all three.

Truly, Jehovah's answer to Abram was vague ("one who will come forth from your own body, he shall be your heir"[22]), but Abram could have asked questions right then, taken the option Isaac took when he prayed for his barren wife, or taken the path Rebekah subsequently took when she had questions and asked God for an explanation about her pregnancy. Further, Abram did not mention Sarai, so neither did Jehovah. What would God have said if Abram had spoken his whole heart and stated, "Sarai and I are childless," instead of "I am childless"?

Thirteen years of "God Hears" and deteriorating relationships later, Jehovah visited with more news: he was going to fix the problem. Abraham, on hearing he would have a son with Sarah, laughed.[23] Then, when Sarah heard, she laughed.[24] Of course God named the resultant son Isaac, meaning laughter. Another continuing reminder of mistakes made.

Again, we have a choice of the types. We can live as a bondwoman, whose progeny are not considered to be part of the kingdom of God, or as a freewoman. And again, Christ has provided the path and example: "For if we have become united with Him in the likeness of His death, certainly we shall also be in the likeness of His resurrection, knowing this, that our old self was crucified with Him, in order that our body of sin might be done away with, so that we would no longer be slaves to sin; for he who has died is freed from sin" (Rom. 6:5–7), and, "For sin shall not be master over you, for you are not under law but under grace" (Rom. 6:14).

We also need reminding that God hears our prayers and that we are in constant danger of not taking Him at His word: "Call to Me and I will answer you, and I will tell you great and mighty things, which you do not know (Jer.33:3). God does the answering and telling in His time and His way. If we are not careful, the answer is so subtle, we miss seeing God in it at all.

Permit a brief digression to amplify this point. Most accounts of the American Revolution include at least one miraculous act of Providence that

21. Gen. 15: 2 and 3.
22. Gen. 15:4.
23. Gen. 17:17.
24. Gen. 18:12.

causes many to conclude God was on the colonist's side. A more detailed accounting, however, shows that the Continental Army was always in dire straits. Shoelessness, hunger, lack of blankets and coats in cold weather, poor pay, and severe lack of guns and ammunition were constant hazards. They barely got by most of the time.

There were a few, even epic, events that made huge differences: a fog at the retreat from Staten Island; a driving snow into the Hessian soldiers' faces (and at the back of the attacking colonists) at Trenton; George Washington never being killed, wounded, or captured despite men dying all around him and snipers not realizing who he was and deciding not to shoot—all these are extraordinary examples. The histories suggest that Providence aided the colonists mainly because victors write the histories.

But I wonder how British historians view these same events. I doubt their conclusion is "God was on their side and so we lost." For them to come to such a conclusion, the Staten Island fog would have had to be unique (at least for that time of year), the snow at Trenton around Christmas always blowing from the opposite direction, and Washington found to be invisible to opposing riflemen. There was never an avenging angel hurling thunderbolts and fire at the enemy.

And yet against incredible hardships and odds, with daily desertions and loyalists' opposition, with the benefit of a series of events that are "fortunate" on their face but taken in toto might be considered God's hand, the Continental Army prevailed.

God hears. He rights oppression. He gives Abraham a son when he and Sarah are so old that the hand of God can not be missed, but God's response to what he hears mostly happens in ways only the people looking to him for answers see.

We laugh. We look at the odds and our resources and think it will not happen as promised. Then comes the birth—a son, a nation, a cause that changes hearts and minds.

The third pair we need to examine is another set of twins, Esau and Jacob. Their story is much more complex than the first two pairs. To start with, their conflict began in utero—they fought. They fought enough that Rebekah sought God out on the matter and received the prophesy that the older shall serve the younger. Rabbi David Fohrman thinks that the struggle in the womb is the sign of a single placenta and sac; i.e., identical twins. At birth they were not identical, however, as a result of the struggle.

One twin had gotten more nutrients and was born "red all over like a hairy garment; and they named him Esau."[25]

The other was born smooth, "and his hand [was] taking hold on Esau's heel, and one calleth his name Jacob."[26] In the Hebrew "they" named Esau, and "he" named Jacob, which means heel or crooked or supplants—not a name to inspire self-confidence. Rebekah must have not liked it, as "he"; i.e., Isaac, did the naming without her.

This paternal favoritism and maternal protection reached a head in the first episode of what Rabbi Fohrman calls Goats and Coats. Esau had traded away his birthright to a brother who had been looking for an opportunity to get it,[27] and had married foreign women, bringing "grief to Isaac and Rebekah."[28] Nevertheless, Isaac determined to give his blessing to the stronger, probably larger, son of the field, Esau, whom Isaac probably saw as the more able of the two sons to carry on the family line.

What happened next is subject to interpretation. R. Fohrman[29] thinks Rebekah wanted Jacob to make a case to Isaac that he was as capable as his brother and deserved the blessing, or at least a blessing. Jacob was resistant, Rebekah persisted, and a compromise was reached with Jacob donning Esau's clothes and some animal skin to add hair.

The exchange between Jacob and Rebekah (verses 27:6–13) needs careful scrutiny. Jacob was concerned about Isaac possibly thinking a deception was afoot and would result in a curse rather than a blessing. R. Fohrman notes that Rebekah's response was based on there being no intended deception: "Your curse be on me, my son; only obey my voice."[30] He thinks Rebekah was shocked when Jacob told Isaac he was Esau, not just his equal as an heir.

It does seem reasonable that no father, even a blind one and maybe especially a blind one, would be fooled by something as superficial as Goats and Coats. Indeed Rashi points to Isaac's response to Jacob's speech as differing from Esau's. In comments on verse 20, noting the response as to how he returned so fast, Rashi writes, "Isaac said to himself, 'It is not Esau's

---

25. Gen. 25:25.

26. Gen. 25:26, Young's Literal Translation

27. This is according to rabbi's interpretation in the Gemara.

28. Gen. 26:35.

29. In *Genesis, a Parsha Companion*, Rabbi Fohrman gives credit for this line of thinking to his mentor, R. Simcha Cook.

30. Gen. 27:13.

way to mention the name of God so readily, and this one says, 'Because the Lord thy God caused it thus to happen to me.'"[31] And again commenting on the way each son addressed Isaac: "because [Jacob] speaks in an entreating strain — "Arise I pray thee." Esau, however, spoke in a harsh strain (v. 31): "Let my father arise."[32]

Looking at the whole situation from Rebekah's point of view, we realize it is not a ruse at all, but a caricature of Isaac's favoritism: all Jacob needed to be Esau was a cloak and some hair. As a plus, Jacob did not have all Esau's baggage.

The struggle between Esau and Jacob, and between Isaac and Rebekah concerning them, had been going on for a long time, possibly eighty years.[33] Surely the parents had discussed Jacob's qualifications and Esau's shortcomings many times. Perhaps when Jacob showed some initiative, Isaac saw him in a different light, as Rebekah had predicted.

R. Fohrman argues that it was not Rebekah's plan for Jacob to claim to be Esau, just that he was at least as capable as Esau; hence she saw no need for a ruse and her lack of concern about any curse. Rashi analyzed the Hebrew and disputed the idea that Jacob claimed to be Esau, citing verse 24: *"and he said I am* — He did not say, 'I am Esau,' but 'It is I,' and in verse 19, *'I am Esau thy first-born* — I am he that brings food to you, and Esau is your first-born.'"

In examining verse 27:23— "[Isaac] did not recognize [Jacob]"— we can conclude that he did not recognize the person before him as the Jacob in whom he had no confidence. The Hebrew word is *nakar*, which also means to acknowledge or know. Possibly Isaac now saw this initiative-taking son differently and did not acknowledge him as the younger son he had underestimated. This son had Esau's hands; i.e., Esau's capabilities, *so* Isaac blessed him.

Rashi, commenting on verse 27:33, writes,

> Why did Isaac tremble? He thought: Perhaps I have sinned in blessing the younger before the elder, thus changing the order of relationship between them. But when Esau began to cry out, "for he hath supplanted me these two times," his father asked him, "What did he do to you?" He replied, "He took away my

---

31. Genesis Rabbah 65:19.

32. Rashi on Genesis. 27, Sefaria.org; Midrash Tanchuma, Toldot 11.

33. Isaac was sixty when they were born, Gen. 25:26; Jacob was with Laban for twenty years; Isaac died at age 180, twenty years after Jacob returned, Gen. 35:28).

birth-right." Isaac thereupon said, "It was on account of this that I was grieved and trembled: perhaps I had overstepped the line of strict justice. Now, however, I have really blessed the first-born — "And he shall indeed be blessed."

Rashi further comments on verse 33 (after Esau returns), concerning whether Isaac was deceived: "*yea, and he shall be blessed* — In order that you may not say 'If Jacob had not deceived his father he would never have received the blessing,' he, therefore, confirmed it, blessing him now of his own free will (Genesis Rabbah 67:2)."[34]

This whole line of reasoning certainly explains Rebekah's statement to Jacob when she told him it was time to run: ". . . flee to Haran, to my brother Laban! Stay with him a few days, until your brother's fury subsides, until your brother's anger against you subsides and he forgets what *you did to him*"[35] (emphasis mine). This coming from a mother who only hours before had said, "Obey *my* voice"[36] (emphasis mine) and told him to carry out the plan she had proposed—and he had opposed.

This is all conjecture, of course. However improbably, maybe Isaac was fooled. He clearly was fooled if he thought he was dying—he lived another two decades.[37]

Again, we have types. Esau was the man of today. When he needed food, he needed it now, and a birthright was way down the list of priorities. When the blessing went to his brother, murder was the answer. He was a bridge burner. Jacob was a future thinker almost to the exclusion of today. He planned and stayed vigilant for the opportunity to gain any birthright or position that would enhance his future. There is no telling how many pots of lentils he cooked before the day his brother came home empty-handed and hungry. Things were going tolerably when he was with Laban, but they could be better, so he made a move. Years later he sent his sons on missions that proved dangerous to them (Joseph to report on his brothers; the brothers to Egypt for grain) because the goal was necessary to secure the future. He built bridges.

Esau and Jacob started life together at impregnation; they separated and they struggled. Each had traits that were valuable but needed tempering

34. Rashi on Genesis 27, sefaria.org.

35. Gen. 27:43–45.

36. Gen. 27:13.

37. Gen. 35:29: He was still alive when Jacob left Laban and returned with two wives and twelve children.

with their gifts. Poor choices that Jacob made in Goats and Coats One had consequences that would be repeated in further Goats and Coats episodes.

In Goats and Coats Two the tables are turned on Jacob. Now he is old and his sons are the deceivers. They give him Joseph's coat, stained with goat's blood, and ask him to identify it. The implied message is, Joseph is dead. Some of Esau's bridge-burning, live-for-today thinking came down on Joseph when he was thrown into the pit, and when the tables turned yet again would befall the devious brothers.

Goats and Coats Three is redemptive. On first reading, it seems the next chapter (Gen. 38) is unrelated to the Joseph saga. While Joseph is chained to a camel headed south, Judah "went down from his brethren, and turned in to a certain Adullamite, whose name was Hirah."[38] The word for "went down" is taken by Rashi to mean a fall from grace in the eyes of his brothers after they saw the grief Judah's plan had caused their father.

Judah hooks up with Tamar, who had changed her widow's garments for a prostitute's shawl; promises of goats are exchanged for services; and a pregnancy and charge of immorality result. When asked to identify his signet ring, cords, and staff that he had given in pledge, as he had asked his father to identify Joseph's coat, Judah dropped deception as a modus operandi: "Judah recognized them, and said, 'She is more righteous than I, since I did not give her to my son Shelah'" (emphasis mine).[39] He took responsibility, saving Tamar and the child, who would become the forefather of King David.

More important to the selling of Joseph saga, the change in Judah would be visible to Jacob when the brothers returned from Egypt with the viceroy's demand to bring Benjamin down. Jacob would not trust Reuben to safeguard Benjamin, but after the lessons of Tamar, Jacob trusted Judah.

In Egypt, when Joseph framed Benjamin for stealing the divination vessels, it was Judah's obvious heart change about Jacob's loving Rachel more than his own mother, Leah, that broke Joseph. Judah put their father's love for Rachel through Benjamin above his own life.[40] When Joseph saw that, he could not maintain his own deception.

In Goats and Coats the deceiver became the deceived until Judah changed. He broke a pattern that had cycled through three generations.

---

38. Gen. 38:1 KJV: or *brothers* EVS. The NASB translates "went down" as departed, but the footnote says literally went down.

39. Gen. 38:26.

40. Gen. 44:25–34.

Jacob became Israel and Israel became slaves. The leadership of Egypt suffered a military change and "a new king arose over Egypt, who did not know Joseph."[41] Conflicts between the Israelite shepherds and the grain merchants of Egypt arose. God heard the outcries and saw the injustices. A choice was laid out to the people: paint your doorposts with lamb's blood or become incorporated into Egypt. The choice was for each family to make; there was no nation of Israel until the following morning.

Once out of Egypt, an escape they sorely wanted, the Israelites found themselves delivered into the wilderness, a resettlement they soon did not want. Staying alive in a desert requires three things: water, food, and shelter.

In Jewish tradition related in the Gemara[42], Moses is associated with the provision of food as he relayed God's messages about manna and quails to the people, while his siblings, Miriam and Aaron, were associated with water (Miriam's well) and shelter (the tabernacle), respectively.

The first of these needs was addressed the first night out of Egypt. The day after the Passover night they "journeyed from Rameses to Succoth."[43] There they stayed in makeshift huts, also called succoth (in Hebrew). It is unclear whether the place derived its name from the dwellings, or the reverse. Nevertheless, God made it safe and provided further protection by "going before them in a pillar of cloud by day to lead them on the way, and in a pillar of fire by night to give them light, that they might travel by day and by night."[44] This protection was the Israelites' constant companion for forty years of desert living.

The second need was addressed three days into the wilderness. They ran out of water.[45] God provided a tree to be thrown into the waters to remove the bitterness at Marah. They had springs at Elim but ran out of water again at Rephidim, where God instructed Moses to strike the rock, causing water to gush out.

---

41. Exod. 1:8.

42. The Gemara is a collection of rabbinical commentaries on the Mishnah. Together they form the Talmud. "Sages in both Babylonia (modern-day Iraq) and the Land of Israel continued to study traditional teachings, including the Mishnah, describing the teachings as having been passed down from Moses at Sinai (either literally or figuratively). The oral discussions were preserved, either by memorization or notation, and later edited together in a manner that places generations of sages in conversation with one another." https://www.myjewishlearning.com/article/gemara-the-essence-of-the-talmud/.

43. Exod. 12:37.

44. Exod. 13:21.

45. Exod. 15:22.

The next time there was a problem with water was forty years later, at the death of Miriam: ". . . and the people stayed at Kadesh. Now Miriam died there and was buried there. There was no water for the congregation, and they assembled themselves against Moses and Aaron."[46]

Consider the improbabilities. Six hundred thousand men left Egypt.[47] Add women and children, and you have at least 1.2 million—a city the size of Dallas. Imagine providing water *and sewer* (more on this later) for Dallas as you moved it around West Texas for forty years—surely this will give you a new prospective on God's provision. The Gemara and Midrash inform us that every time the Israelites would stop to camp, Miriam's well—the rock Moses had struck which was shaped like a sieve and rolled along when the cloud moved the camp—would dig into the sand, then the leaders of the tribes would shout, "Rise up, O well," and enough water for Dallas would rise up.[48]

The third need for desert dwellers, food, did not come up until six weeks after the Israelites left Egypt, presumably after they had used up all their stores of wheat and animals.[49] (They would be provided food, their tents and clothes wouldn't wear out eliminating the need of skins or wool, and sanitation/grazing became easier.) The Gemara also notes that manna was fully absorbed, requiring no sewer.

Besides the association of desert needs to the desert leaders mentioned above, I want to outline parallels to the three sets of brothers we are discussing in this section. The pairs represent lessons God is trying to instill in His people; the desert provides final test of those lessons before the people are admitted back into the Promised Land.

As we know, the third generation[50]—those born in Egypt but dying in the desert—did not pass the test. The fourth generation—those born in the desert and dying in the Promised Land—would fulfill the twofold promise of land and descendants from Genesis 15 (as God told Abraham they would).

First, shelter. As we just saw, this was dealt with first and corresponds to our first pair of brothers. There was a curse on the land, and Abel wanted no part of it. The curse was a result of disobedience—of seeking to fulfill

46. Num. 20: 1 and 2.

47. Exod. 12:37.

48. Midrash, Bamidbar Rabbah 1:1.

49. Exod. 16.

50. See Appendix B, The Spiritual Generations of Israel.

"the lust of the flesh, the lust of the eyes, and the boastful pride of life [which] is not from the Father but is from the world."[51] Abel had distanced himself far enough from his parents' mistake that his offering was accepted. It is curious to note that we hear nothing of the first parents making offerings when their sons are bringing theirs. You would think that if they had brought acceptable offerings, we would have heard about it.

Cain failed. He not only failed in his offering but also failed after a warning that sin was waiting for him. He did not seem to care, maybe as his parents did not care. It is interesting that he brought an offering at all. Maybe some fruit was harvested unripe, and he threw it on the fire and said a prayer. We do not know. He was new to offerings.

We do know there is a parallel in the early Christian church. Some in Corinth were taking communion without first evaluating their heart attitudes:

> For as often as you eat this bread and drink the cup, you proclaim the Lord's death until He comes. Therefore whoever eats the bread or drinks the cup of the Lord in an unworthy manner, shall be guilty of the body and the blood of the Lord. But a man must examine himself, and in so doing he is to eat of the bread and drink of the cup. For he who eats and drinks, eats and drinks judgment to himself if he does not judge the body rightly. For this reason many among you are weak and sick, and a number sleep. But if we judged ourselves rightly, we would not be judged (1 Cor. 11:26–31).

What was missing in Corinth was missing in Eden, and what was missing east of Eden was penance—a heart of reconciliation. Cain would rather fight the ground and live on his own terms than be reconciled to God. As a result, things simply got worse. People in Corinth died physically, and Cain was on his way to a spiritual death.[52]

Israel was driven out of Egyptian cities into the desert where for forty years they lived in tents, like their father Abraham. His grandson, Jacob, is described as "a complete man, living in tents."[53] The nomadic life in tents forces you to limit your possessions.

---

51. 1 John. 2:16.

52. See Section 2, cycle 3 for a discussion of Cain's possible change of heart and the result.

53. Gen. 25:27 NASB: see marginal note.

Another complete man living a nomadic life was Paul. He went from city to city spreading the Gospel and planting churches. He worked with his hands to provide for himself wherever he was, but his lifestyle prevented him from accumulating possessions. He was always on call to God. He never knew when he would be sent out of an Antioch or called to a Macedonia. He might stay many months in Corinth, a few weeks in Thessalonica, or only days before being driven out of Berea.

Because he "lived in tents" he could write to the Philippians that in spite of his many accomplishments in the religious community, "whatever things were gain to me, those things I have counted as loss for the sake of Christ."[54] In the Greek, *gain* is plural but *loss* is singular—many "possessions" given up in one loss were, for Paul, as it should be for us, "that I may know Him and the power of His resurrection and the fellowship of His sufferings, being conformed to His death; in order that I may attain to the resurrection from the dead."[55]

In Matthew 13 Jesus tells of a man who was wandering in a field and finds a treasure. He sold all that he had to buy the field. His point is that we should be looking for opportunities to give up all our possessions to gain the kingdom of heaven. But let us think a minute about what happened next. We know the man had done well enough to have the assets to buy a field. We also know that he had some of the effects of the curse in his heart: he was trespassing in his neighbor's field; he hid the treasure he had discovered; he certainly did not disclose the existence of the treasure. (Worse case: he was out there at night looking for treasure.)

The point of the parable is still valid, but if our hearts are unrenewed, what started out as a treasure could become a life-consuming project if we are not constantly on guard against that happening. The true treasure of the kingdom of God is a renewed heart.

The first lesson of the desert is that it is not enough to get Israel out of Egypt; God had to get the pride of Egyptian living out of Israel. Ten plagues were not enough. Seeing the waters open and then swallow the Egyptian army was not enough. Living in tents for forty years was not enough. The third generation died in the wilderness.

It is better to obey in the little things than to try to live under a curse.

The middle part of the five books of the Pentateuch—the last half of Exodus, all of Leviticus, and the first half of Numbers—is about the

54. Phil. 3:7.
55. Phil. 3:10b–11.

tabernacle. The tabernacle was a holy space for God in the middle of the safe space God was providing for Israel. With the tabernacle God established a procedure for penance. Though the sacrifice was very personal, the one seeking reconciliation had to walk through the whole camp, in full view of every prying eye. He could not sneak in either—he had a bull with him.

Priests were assigned to assist the penitent, and provisions were made for the poor—no one was excluded from God's altar. The tabernacle and sacrifices provided a mechanism for people to keep short accounts with God and man with the focus always on the heart attitude.

Living under the curse causes us to gather enough stuff around us to make living under the curse tolerable. Between gathering and protecting what we gather, our lives can be consumed. God is calling us out from under the curse into the heart of a tent-dweller.

The second need in the desert is water. Miriam is associated with water because most times water is mentioned, she is there. Starting with her brother being placed in the Nile as an infant, through her dance of victory at the Red Sea (she had prophesied that her brother would lead them out of Egyptian bondage, so her dance was a victory lap), passively at the bitter waters of Marah by virtue of her name being derived from *marah*, even to her death when the water stopped flowing, the gift of water in the desert was seen as due to Miriam's merit.

The exodus started with Israel crying out to God from their bondage. God wanted them to know that he heard their cries. He knew about the slavery. He knew about the babies being drowned in the Nile. His instructions to Moses and the sending of ten plagues were designed to deliver the message to Israel (and Pharaoh) that God hears, God knows. The message was repeated when the waters parted,[56] when the bitterness resolved at Marah, when Moses struck the rock at Rephidim, and at every encampment when the elders repeated, "Rise up, O well." God hears.

Matthew tells a story in his Gospel about the disciples crossing the Sea of Galilee at night while Jesus stayed behind dismissing the crowds and praying.[57] The winds were adverse (or hostile), and the boat was battered by waves. The word translated battered can mean torture or vex with

56. It is interesting that the waters parting happened twice—the Red Sea and Jericho—but both were seen only by Joshua and Caleb.

57. Matt. 14:22–33.

grievous pains, so these were serious waves. The men got in the boat around sundown and were still struggling to cross the sea at three AM. They were tired, probably hungry, and, at least the non-fishermen among them, scared. Then things got worse. They saw a ghost, and it was coming for them. "They were terrified" (Matt. 14:26).

Jesus knew they were afraid and "spoke to them, saying, 'Take courage, it is I; do not be afraid.'" Of course, that is exactly what any ghost worth his salt would say, so Peter, an old salt himself, devised a plan.

"Lord, if it is You, command me to come to You on the water."

"Come."

The story is well known. Peter begins to walk, gets distracted by the storm winds, and starts to sink. Jesus grabs him, gets him back to the boat, and the wind stops.

Three points need our attention. First, what was Jesus thinking as he got Peter back to the boat? Network News would have shown film of Peter sinking and having to be rescued. They would show shots of him sitting alone, dejected, soaking wet and shivering with a blanket wrapped around him. I bet Jesus did not see failure at all. He pointed out the obvious doubt, but this was pre-Pentecost. Peter was still in training. He did have the foresight to ask Jesus to command him to get out of the boat. The Greek word translated "command" means just that, "command." And, accordingly, Peter got out of the boat. True, he needed a little assistance getting back in, but in the middle of a calamity he was walking with Jesus.

Second is to note that despite howling winds and crashing waves, Jesus heard the disciples as they "cried out in fear." As long as they concentrated on him, they were communicating.

Third is a gut check. Place yourself in the boat. If Peter had made it and was standing in the waves with Jesus, who do you think would have gone next? (I bet on John.) More importantly, how many disciples would have gotten out of the boat and walked on the water before you went?

Peter sank because of doubt. Where is your heart when you are taking a battering and your best effort is getting you nowhere?

Water provided a "cleansing" at the Red Sea where Israel was as good as dead with the Egyptian chariots chasing them into the sea, and was alive anew as they came out on the other side with their (physical) enemies destroyed. The miracle waters again destroyed their enemies in the valley of the Amorites (see Num. 21: 15–20).

Israel was miraculously baptized into Moses' leadership at the Red Sea and into Joshua's at the Jordan. Each time, the old was put away and the new taken up.

So it is today with the sacrament of baptism:

> Therefore we have been buried with Him through baptism into death, so that as Christ was raised from the dead through the glory of the Father, so we too might walk in newness of life. For if we have become united with Him in the likeness of His death, certainly we shall also be in the likeness of His resurrection, knowing this, that our old self was crucified with Him, in order that our body of sin might be done away with, so that we would no longer be slaves to sin (Rom. 6:4–6).

Israel in the desert had a miraculous experience with water, and so do we through baptism. God hears our cries and has provided a means of escape from the bondage of sin. I need to accept the atonement as a gift like water in the desert.

The third desert requirement is food. God provided food in the desert in a unique way, not that the tabernacle and Miriam's well were not unique, but wells and tents had been seen before. When the manna first appeared, the response was, "What is it?" Hence, the name. As mentioned before, it was a total food—complete nutrition and completely absorbed.

Manna was also designed to inculcate the lessons of our third pair of siblings. Where Jacob mortgaged the day at hand and focused on the future, the manna was gathered only for the present—it could not be stored. Jacob's descendants learned daily reliance on Jehovah's care for forty years.[58] There was no birthright to procure or blessing to obtain by hook or crook. The manna was new every morning.

Esau thought in terms of present needs, and those needs were largely driven by greed, something incompatible with the spirit in which God gave manna. For those in the desert the manna came with lessons. First, greed was discouraged: "When they measured it with an omer, he who had gathered much had no excess, and he who had gathered little had no lack; every man gathered as much as he should eat."[59] Second, hoarding was forbidden: "Moses said to them, "Let no man leave any of it until morning. But they did not listen to Moses, and some left part of it until morning, and

58. Exod. 16:35, Josh. 5:12.
59. Exod. 16:18.

it bred worms and became foul."[60] Third, if you wanted to eat, you had to crawl out of bed and get to work: "They gathered it morning by morning, every man as much as he should eat; but when the sun grew hot, it would melt."[61] Fourth, they were to remember the Sabbath day and keep it holy: "on the sixth day they gathered twice as much bread, two omers for each one. [Moses] said to them, 'This is what the LORD meant: Tomorrow is a sabbath observance, a holy sabbath to the LORD. Bake what you will bake and boil what you will boil, and all that is left over put aside to be kept until morning.'" Fifth was the lesson of humility: "He humbled you and let you be hungry and fed you with manna which you did not know, nor did your fathers know, that He might make you understand that man does not live by bread alone, but man lives by everything that proceeds out of the mouth of the LORD."[62]

It is true that "In the beginning God created the heavens and the earth," but he did not create everything he could create; he has things behind the curtain. Manna was one of them. A suffering Savior, an empty tomb, and Pentecost would be coming. Sanctification of the believer is new every morning to this day.

In his Gospel, John relates a story about Jesus resting at a well in Sychar, Samaria,[63] while the disciples went to town for food.[64] Why all twelve needed to go for groceries is not explained, except Jesus clearly had a divine appointment with a Samaritan woman that day at that well.

When the disciples returned, a lot had changed. A stray waterpot was by the well, and the men of the village were coming with questions about the Christ. And Jesus, despite the morning's walk through the hills and the break for lunch, was not hungry. All he was interested in were the people from town who were hurrying to him based on what the woman had told them. "Meanwhile the disciples were urging Him, saying, 'Rabbi, eat.' But He said to them, 'I have food to eat that you do not know about.'" Undoubtedly the disciples were confused at first but then learned of the Samarian woman and spiritual food.

---

60. Exod. 16:20.

61. Exod. 16:21.

62. Deut. 8:3.

63. The town and Jacob's well are still there and attract thousands of pilgrims annually.

64. John 4:4–32.

The thing is, many times God is sending angels with spiritual food, but perhaps you're like me. I want a hamburger. I crave the fries. I am planning what flavor of milkshake to get. Spiritual food is not always where my head is.

A Hebrew born about the time the exodus caravan reached Mt. Horeb, over the time until they crossed the Jordan River into the Promised Land, could look forward to 14,600 straight days of manna. Every so often as they boiled, fried, dried, poached, or baked it, someone would bring up the quail meal they'd had way back, but little Levi missed that. Manna, manna, manna. Yes, it showed up every day; yes, they did not have to worry about constipation, diarrhea, gluten sensitivity, scurvy, atherosclerosis, iron deficiency, food allergies, or diabetes, but every day was the same: manna.

God is still providing my daily food. If he did not make rain, there would be a drought and the crops would wither. If he did not make the sun, there would be no photosynthesis and nothing would grow. But still, I confess, I want to feel that I'm in charge. I eat what I want and do not know any more about spiritual food than those disciples sitting by Jacob's well tossing pebbles at the water jar.

But Jesus was not through with the education of his disciples, as he is not through with me. "While they were eating, Jesus took some bread, and after a blessing, He broke it and gave it to the disciples, and said, 'Take, eat; this is my body.' And when he had taken a cup and given thanks, he gave it to them, saying, 'Drink from it, all of you; for this is my blood of the covenant, which is poured out for many for forgiveness of sins.'"[65]

The exodus into the desert brought lessons: Miriam's well bringing water, the tabernacle and its unique laws, and the manna. He also used pairs of contrasting sons to illustrate these lessons. God started with one man, Adam, and one woman, Eve, and ordained that the earth be populated, but he was not in a hurry. Whereas the patriarchs could have had many children—most of the early people did—he used three pairs of sons to bring our attention to key lessons. He even had two resets when the lessons were not being learned: eight people got off the ark, and Abram was called away from his family for new beginnings.

The final tune-up in the wilderness before bringing his people back into the Promised Land reiterated the lessons of the patriarchs. When the Israelites still had not learned them, they experienced yet another reset. The third generation was buried in the sand, and only those born and raised with the rules of the desert, with the tabernacle, Miriam's well, and the manna would come to the Jordan. There they crossed over as the waters

---

65. Matt. 26:26–28.

once again parted for their own baptism, just as they had in the exodus stories told by their parents. It was their own new beginning. Like Noah, like Abram, and like their parents. Had they absorbed the lessons?

"These things happened as examples for us, so that we would not crave evil things as they indeed craved them."[66]

Consider the parallels and contrasts below:

Abel and Cain	Ishmael and Isaac	Esau and Jacob
Relationship to curse	God hears	Today vs. tomorrow
Tabernacle	Miriam's well	Manna
Shelter/provision	Water	Food
Penance	Baptism	Eucharist

The basic assumption of penance, one of the sacraments in Catholicism, is a recognition of sin's curse in my life. Not Adam's sin; not generic, vague, hereditary sin of man, but my sin which I have committed that has separated me from Jehovah. I see the curse and I do not want to live with it anymore.

The basic assumption of baptism is that God hears my plea of identification with the cross of Christ, with his death that should have been mine. God hears me when I say that I "have been buried with Him through baptism into death, so that as Christ was raised from the dead through the glory of the Father, so [I] too might walk in newness of life."[67]

The basic assumption of the Eucharist is that "he who eats My flesh and drinks My blood abides in Me, and I in him."[68] I become a "slave for obedience . . . resulting in sanctification, and the outcome, eternal life."[69] As a result, I have no agenda but God's agenda, no plan but God's plan.

Once again, we recall the insightful words of Oswald Chambers that began this section:

> "A distinction must always be made between the revelation of Redemption and the conscious experience of salvation in a man's life."[70]

---

66. 1 Cor. 10:6.

67. Rom. 6:4.

68. John 6:56.

69. Rom. 6:16 and 22

70. Chambers, *My Utmost for His Highest,* October 7.

Lessons cannot simply be understood; they must be internalized. This is the lesson of the brothers in Genesis, of Israel in the wilderness, and of the sacraments we partake of today.

Section 4

Structure of the Pentateuch and Related Topics

The Sailhamer Synthesis

THE PENTATEUCH IS A single work that historically and conveniently has been divided into five books. Fully understanding any of the five requires understanding its place in the whole. Large books have been written describing the complex interweaving of the stories—one passage presaging a coming section, inclusion of near identical stories, some of the parts out of chronological order. The intent of this section is to get an overview that allows us a sense of the depth without getting caught in complexity as intellectual exercise.

John Sailhamer, in the excellent introduction to his book *The Pentateuch as Narrative,* describes the recurrent structural techniques of the Pentateuch as (1) a *story* section followed by (2) a *poetic* break, and then (3) a brief *epilogue.* The first example of this is the story of creation in Genesis 1:12–22, then an exclamation by Adam that Eve is "bone of my bones" in Genesis 2:23,[1] followed by the Genesis 2:24 summary "for this cause . . ."

Story	Poetry	Epilogue
In the beginning. . .	Bone of my bones. . .	For this cause. . .

This basic unit is repeated to build Genesis chapters one through forty-eight. Genesis forty-nine is Israel's prophecy concerning his family, which is the poetic climax for the whole book and is followed by a tidying up epilogue section—Genesis 49:28 through Exodus 1:6, which includes Israel and Joseph's deaths and burials.

---

1. The poetic sections are set apart in a different format or font in some Bibles.

The Story of the Patriarchs			Poetry	Epilogue
Story	Poetry	Epilogue	Gen. 49 Israel's prophecy	Gen. 50
Gen. 1–2:22	Gen. 2:23	Gen. 2:24–25		
Gen. 3:1–13	Gen.3:14–19	Gen. 3:20–24		
Gen. 4:1–22	Gen. 4:23–24	Gen. 4:25–26		
Continuing through Gen. 48				

This structural technique is next enlarged into a super-structure as Genesis, Exodus, Leviticus, and most of Numbers become the story of the beginnings and trials of God's people in Egypt and leaving Egypt, and of covenants made, expanded, and ignored. The prophecy of Balaam in Numbers 24 is the poem, followed by an epilogue in Numbers 25 with a census in Numbers 26 (similar to the numbering in the Genesis epilogue in Exod. 1:1–6 which, as Sailhamer points out, belongs with Genesis).

Story: Getting Egypt out of Israel			Poetry	Epilogue
Story	Poetry	Epilogue	Num. 23 and 24 Balaam's Prophesy	Num. 25 and 26 Census
Gen. 1–48	Gen. 49	Gen. 50		
Exod. 1–14	Exod. 15:1–21	Exod. 15:22		
Continuing through Num. 22				

Mega-structure is developed as all the Pentateuch to Deuteronomy thirty-one incorporates the wilderness narrative as the story; Deuteronomy thirty-two and thirty-three—The Song of Moses and the Blessing of Moses—is the poetic section; Deuteronomy thirty-four a finishing epilogue relating the death of Moses.

Story: Choose Life			Poetry	Epilogue
Story	Poetry	Epilogue	Deut. 32 and 33 Song of Moses	Deut. 34
Gen. 1–48	Gen. 49	Gen. 50		
Exod. 1–14	Exod.15:1–21	Exod. 15:22		
Exod. 16–Num. 22	Num. 23 and 24	Num. 25 and 26		
Num. 27 through Deut. 31				

Sailhamer also points out that the "seams" between the story and the poem in each of the three larger structural units contain another structural element. The poet *gathers* his audience (Gen. 49:1, Num. 24:14, and Deut.

31:28) and proclaims *what will happen* in the *days to come* (Genesis and Numbers) or *latter days* (Numbers and Deuteronomy).[2]

Why these structural techniques? Because they are memorial. We communicate traditions, truths, and heritage to each other by recounting stories. We remember people more by their adventures than by dates and treaties. We can also relate concepts by analogy. Jean-Babtiste Fourrer, counsel to Napoleon, showed that analogy—essentially the recognition of similar paradigms in different fields—is among the most powerful modes of thought.[3] Paul, for instance, used analogies from the law to justify paying a preacher of the Gospel.[4]

Similarly, we remember poems. In the first poetic example above, "bone of my bone," even the casual Bible reader can add the next phrase from memory.[5] If a group of twenty (the number required is less if older people are in the group) is asked, as I have done, "What day did Paul Revere make his ride?" someone will respond "the eighteenth of April in 1775." Asked how they remembered it, they will say, "Well, there's a poem about it," and perhaps remember Henry W. Longfellow's famous lines:

> Gather, my children, and you shall hear
> Of the midnight ride of Paul Revere
> *On the eighteenth of April, in Seventy-Five*
> Hardly a man is now alive
> Who remembers that famous day and year!

The date (emphasized in line three) is remembered as much because of Longfellow as Revere.

These structural elements, and many more beyond our purposes here but available to those interested in the books cited, point to a powerful, unified literary strategy in the Pentateuch. Far from being a patched-together collection of Hebrew myths, it has a purpose and message that goes much deeper than the individual stories. The more effort taken to ferret out the techniques, the greater the realization of the care that went into their formulation.

---

2. Depending on which translation is being used.

3. George Gilder, *Telecosm*, 210. Fourrer noted the analogy between heat moving through a metal bar and the convertibility of wave action between the time and frequency domains, an example of complex concepts being understood through their similarity to easily understood concepts.

4. 1 Cor. 9:9

5. "and flesh of my flesh," Gen. 2:23.

Selection as Revelation

TEMPTING AS IT IS to take the Pentateuch as the complete early history of Israel from the creation to approaching the Promised Land or, as Irish Archbishop James Ussher did in 1650, to assign a date to the beginning of creation based on the genealogies and years stated in the text,[1] it is not possible. The Pentateuch is not and cannot be a blow-by-blow account of every event of the timeframe covered. It is a selection of events and conversations from all the events and conversations that occurred.

The genealogies do not claim to be complete. Take a look at Matthew's genealogy as he starts his Gospel. He divides Jewish history from Abraham to Jesus into three sections of fourteen men each, but to create this symmetry he leaves out many sons and fathers documented in Kings and Chronicles, and includes David in two sections. Clearly the symmetry of the genealogy is more important than all-inclusive, exact historical correctness.

Egyptian genealogies go back farther in time than allowed by Genesis; the Chinese go back even farther. "Who is right about the timeframe?" is not the right question. "Why are we told what we are told?" gets at the issue. The genealogies have purposes other than documentation of family lines.

This can be understood further by looking at the first genealogy, Genesis 2:4: "These are the generations of the heavens and of the earth when they were created, in the day that the LORD God made the earth and the heavens" (KJV). "Generations" is translated as "births" in Young's Literal Translation. The word is *towldah*,[2] which means family, lineage, genealogy. Note that this genealogy is of *the heavens and the earth*—not people.

---

1. Namely, at twilight, Sunday, Oct. 23, 4004 BC.
2. *Strong's* H8435.

Clearly the Pentateuch looks at genealogies differently than, say, Mormons do. The lists convey information we need, just not an exact reproduction of generations for dating purposes.

The selection in the genealogies is the revelation. Gaps in time occur during which God might have been silent, but if he spoke, we are not told what was said. All we know is that we don't need information about the gap. For example, in Genesis 16:16 we read, "Abram was eighty-six," as compared to the next verse, Genesis 17:1: "Abram was ninety-nine." Many times, as discussed in Section two, prior events and conversations are implied, leaving out the when and why.

In Genesis 14:22, Abram said to the king of Sodom," I have sworn to the LORD God Most High, possessor of heaven and earth, that I will not take a thread or a sandal thong or anything that is yours, for fear you would say, 'I have made Abram rich.'" When did he swear that oath? Was it when he was coming out of Egypt? After defeating the four kings? We are not told and do not need to know. Abram made the commitment, and he stuck to it.

Care must be taken to infer all that can safely be learned, always asking ourselves why, if some piece of information can safely be inferred, are we left to do the inferring and not told outright? Most of the time the answer is that God wants us thinking deeply about the stories; to reflect on ancient mysteries "hidden since the foundation of the world"[3] that are contained there; to allow the ferreting process to turn our hearts toward God—which is precisely the point.

So, for instance, when you notice that Leviticus fails to provide a complete set of rules for worship, analyze *why* we are given what is in the text rather than throwing out Leviticus because of what is not included. What is provided gives us plenty to try to understand.

There are two great themes of the Pentateuch: creation and salvation. Genesis chapters one and two lay out the creation, but as discussed above, the creation story sets the foundation for much more than just the rest of the Pentateuch. The exodus is an obvious type of salvation, but a closer reading shows that salvation is the theme of Genesis chapters five, seven, twelve, fourteen, nineteen, and twenty-two as well.

Further, these two great themes— "I created you" and "I saved you"— are equated. With this in mind, consider the two listings of the Ten Commandments, Exodus 20 and Deuteronomy 5. The versions are identical, except for the fourth commandment.

3. Matt. 13:35.

The Exodus version states;

> Remember the Sabbath day, to keep it holy. Six days you shall la-
> bor and do all your work, but the seventh day is a Sabbath of the
> LORD your God; in it you shall not do any work, you or your son
> or your daughter, your male or your female servant or your cattle
> or your sojourner who stays with you. *For in six days the LORD
> made the heavens and the earth, the sea and all that is in them, and
> rested on the seventh day;* therefore the LORD blessed the Sabbath
> day and made it holy (emphasis mine). [4]

The Deuteronomy version is identical until the rationale statement:

> "*You shall remember that you were a slave in the land of Egypt,
> and the LORD your God brought you out of there by a mighty hand
> and by an outstretched arm;* therefore the LORD your God com-
> manded you to observe the Sabbath day (emphasis mine). [5]

These two great events, displaying God's power and purpose, are used
to justify the same command: "Remember the Sabbath day, to keep it holy."
We are to keep the Sabbath holy, separated to God, by the command of our
Creator and our Savior.

---

4. Exod. 20:8-11.

5. Deut. 5:12–15.

Sub-Optimization

UNDERSTANDING THE CONCEPT OF sub-optimization is extremely useful in guiding us through the spiritual, moral, and historical stories of the Pentateuch. Sub-optimization is an attempt to optimize the end position of sub-units of the whole without lessening the outcome for the whole. Mostly, it can't be done. According to Robert A. Frosch, quoted in the Merriam-Webster online dictionary, "optimization of a particular process or subsystem . . . may be less efficient than optimization of the larger-scale system." Whereas optimization of any one or few sub-units is easy, the result is frequently detrimental to the whole.

A quick illustration of sub-optimization is the story of the wolf pack. It is optimal for any one wolf to wait for the pack to kill a moose and then join in the feast—all benefit, no danger or energy loss. If more wolves join him on the sideline, however, the remainder of the pack cannot bring down a moose, and all go hungry. As it is difficult for wolves working alone to stay in food (they don't do well catching rabbits or other game they can bring down alone), attempts at sub-optimization—in other words, maximum benefits to that one wolf—fail.

The Prisoner's Dilemma, a problem developed in the 1950s by the Rand Corporation and a mainstay of game theory, is one of many iterations demonstrating this point.[1] One version of the Prisoner's Dilemma is that two ex-cons are arrested for robbery resulting in the homeowner being severely injured. At the time of arrest both men are found with guns, which

---

1. I mention it here to cue anyone more interested in the concept to find it on Google. The concept of sub- optimization resonates with some people but is confusing to others.

are parole violations, but there is nothing to place the two at the scene of the burglary.

Each man is approached separately and each is told he would be going back to prison on the parole violation for say ten years. The men are also told that if they turn state's evidence against the other prisoner about the robbery, their time could be reduced to three years, and that if the other guy turns on him first, he will get twenty-five years for the robbery and assault.

The prisoner's dilemma is this: if prisoner one sub-optimizes for his best outcome, he should turn state's evidence. He gets the light sentence—three years; but prisoner two gets twenty-five years, and the pair do twenty-eight years combined. Of course, if he says nothing and prisoner two turns, the roles are reversed. If both prisoners give evidence against the other, they both get twenty-five years. The best case for each man (sub-optimization) is that he rat on his friend, hoping the friend stays loyal to him. The best case for the pair is for neither to say a thing. The worst case is that they both cave. There is no way get a better result for one without affecting the whole adversely.

The reader can easily get caught up in the individual circumstances of the players of the Pentateuch, say Abram—particularly Abram—and fall into second-guessing his decisions, forgetting Abram's submission to God, who is orchestrating a much bigger stage than we are being shown at any one time. Types are being placed which foreshadow events hundreds of years forward, requiring actions that can be criticized individually but are necessary when observed as part of the whole.

We have discussed the journey of Abram and Sarai into Egypt, Sarai's enslavement in Pharaoh's harem, God's resultant judgment on Pharaoh, and the couple's deliverance, which foreshadows Israel's journey to Egypt, their enslavement, and God's judgment and deliverance. This in turn fore-shadows our individual present-day journeys into "Egypt" and slavery to sin and need for deliverance. For now, it is enough to say that to set a type for slavery in a foreign land requires slaves, many of whom cannot point to a bad decision or major mistake that landed them in such dire straits and who are not privy to the big picture as we now are, but nevertheless are making bricks in Egypt. They are the sub-unit in a less than an enviable situation but positioned to optimize the whole.

The Pentateuch Forward

THE REST OF THE Pentateuch, including the Passover and the exodus, is how the law was given and used. It came in pieces. With each failure God gave more law. This opens two possible interpretations about what was going on. The first is law-as-burden—God punishing Israel with the law; the more they rebel, the more punishment they deserve and the more they get. The law, as we all know and know and know, cannot save anyone.[1] The law increases sin[2] and brings punishment on those who try to obey it.[3] The law arouses evil desires[4] and enslaves us to sin.[5] The law is a burden.

The second interpretation is law-as-tutor. According to this understanding the extra laws are not meant as punishment; they are not increased to punish rebellion but helpful additions to correct hearts that rebel. God is good and holy and righteous, and he gave his people a law that is good and holy and righteous.[6] God chose this people, Israel, revealed his glory to them, made covenants and promises, and allowed them the privilege of worshipping him.[7] He also gave them a law they could not keep but which would lead them to the One who could.

The trouble is not with the law, but with the keepers.[8] It is not a means of salvation but a means of demonstrating the need for salvation:

1. Rom. 3:20.
2. Rom. 8:3.
3. Rom. 4:15. This is not the same as the law itself being punishment.
4. Rom. 7:5.
5. Rom. 6:14.
6. Rom. 7:12.
7. Rom. 9:4.
8. Rom. 7:14.

For the law of the Spirit of life in Christ Jesus has set you free from the law of sin and of death. For what the Law could not do, weak as it was through the flesh, God did: sending His own Son in the likeness of sinful flesh and as an offering for sin, He condemned sin in the flesh, so that the requirement of the Law might be fulfilled in us, who do not walk according to the flesh but according to the Spirit. [9]

And this: "The Law has become our tutor to lead us to Christ, so that we may be justified by faith."[10] The law, our tutor, and the Holy Spirit, our Helper, are to have the same result in us—lead us through repentance to Christ.

Jesus admonished the teachers of the law: "You search the Scriptures because you think that in them you have eternal life; it is these that testify about Me."[11] He further states, "For My yoke is easy and *My burden is light*"[12] (emphasis mine). It seems that the more we see the law-as-tutor, accept its purpose, and allow it to draw us to Christ, the less law-as-burden it becomes.

The Scriptures that testify of Christ, particularly the Pentateuch and more specifically the law, are a long analogy. The law deals with how to live, how to have relationships—first with God, secondly with his people, then with strangers among us, and finally with everyone else. The Pentateuch is a case history of Israel's successes and failures in those relationships—especially with Jehovah Jireh, revealed to Abraham on Moriah and forgotten by Israel in the desert.

There is something else. Think back to the events in the garden in Eden. Compare Adam before the fall to Abraham whom we traced from Ur to Moriah. What was the difference?

Adam was in a place made as perfect as God could make it. The first man was to keep the garden, but there was no sin and no curse, those things that seem to make everything hard today. There were no sexual temptations to distract him, no money worries, no marauding tribes threatening his life. But there was a flaw in Eden: Adam's heart. He had been given everything, but he had not been tested. He walked with God because that is what

9. Rom. 8:2–4.

10. Gal. 3:24.

11. John 5:39

12. Matt. 11:30.

you do in Eden; God showed up, they walked. I'm not implying that Adam didn't want to walk with God, but he didn't know anything else.

Abraham, on the other hand, made choice after choice to walk with God. He left his family, something that might even appeal to you right now depending on your circumstances, but it was not the thing done in the culture of the time. He was leaving one of the most advanced civilizations of the day to go . . . where? Abraham was brought along through stages, including long times of no contact with Jehovah, to the foot of a mountain far from home with his miracle son, two servants, a donkey, and a pile of wood. Laying the wood on the son and starting up the mountain was a choice of faith. Laying the son on the wood and raising his knife was an act of supreme faith; he would rather have raised the knife for his own death.

I submit that God prefers Genesis 22 to Genesis 2. One day he will restore us to something not unlike Eden, but it will be populated by saints with tested hearts who are there because they made a choice of faith.

Solomon, like Adam, had an ideal situation. Wealth, power, reputation, wisdom, and women all were his in abundance, but he could see ""Vanity of vanities! All is vanity"[13] and, "I considered all my activities which my hands had done and the labor which I had exerted and behold all was vanity and striving after wind and there was no profit under the sun."[14]

That is not what Abraham would say. He would say, "I know Jehovah Jireh, and He is faithful and true. All he has said he has done to me and I am his."

That would be Abraham, the Father of Faith, speaking from a tutored, trained, tested heart. He can be the subject of a debate as to whether he was man or myth, or he can be a guiding light to lead you into faith and righteousness. Choose Life.

"Now these things happened to them as an example, and they were written for our instruction, upon whom the ends of the ages have come" (1 Cor. 10:11).

---

13. Eccles. 1:2.
14. Eccles. 2:11.

Appendix A

The Bible Without Genesis?

IF WE THINK THE Old Testament is a collection of myths and folk stories or about an old God who was full of wrath, and we want to use the New Testament exclusively for its teachings about Jesus and His love, we have a major problem. The New Testament writers believed the Old Testament and incorporated its teaching into their accounts and letters.

Below are examples of those writers' use of Old Testament quotes or teaching. If we cannot trust the Old Testament, we cannot trust the New Testament writers who did trust it, nor can we trust their books. To eliminate the "untrustworthy" New Testament books with direct Old Testament references leaves very little, and that little becomes almost nothing if we eliminate the authors who are suspect because of their reliance on the Old Testament? (If Paul is wrong in Ephesians, why should Galatians be trusted?) The list is not exhaustive but makes the point with representative examples. The italics are mine, added for emphasis, and I have included only representative quotes from New Testament writers to illustrate their Old Testament reliance and belief.

MATTHEW 19:4–5: "And He answered and said, 'Have you not read that *He who created them from the beginning made them male and female, and said, 'for this reason* a man shall leave his father and mother and be joined to his wife, and the two shall become one flesh'?"

MARK 10:6–8: "But *from the beginning of creation, God made them male and female. For this reason* a man shall leave his father and mother, and the two shall become one flesh; so they are no longer two, but one flesh."

LUKE 24:25–27: "And He said to them, "O foolish men and slow of heart to believe in all that the prophets have spoken! Was it not necessary for the Christ to suffer these things and to enter into His glory? Then *beginning with Moses and with all the prophets, He explained to them the things concerning Himself in all the Scriptures.*"

JOHN 1:1–4: "In the beginning was the Word, and the Word was with God, and the Word was God. He was in the beginning with God. *All things came into being through Him, and apart from Him nothing came into being that has come into being.* In Him was life, and the life was the Light of men."

ACTS 17:24–26: "The *God who made the world and all things in it, since He is Lord of heaven and earth, does not dwell in temples made with hands;* nor is He served by human hands, as though He needed anything, since He Himself gives to all people life and breath and all things; and He made from one man every nation of mankind to live on all the face of the earth, having determined their appointed times and the boundaries of their habitation."

ROMANS 1:20: "*For since the creation of the world His invisible attributes, His eternal power and divine nature, have been clearly seen, being understood through what has been made, so that they are without excuse.*"

1 CORINTHIANS 11:7: "For *a man ought not to have his head covered, since he is the image and glory of God*; but the woman is the glory of man."

2 CORINTHIANS 4:6: "*For God, who said, 'Light shall shine out of darkness,'* is the One who has shone in our hearts to give the Light of the knowledge of the glory of God in the face of Christ."

EPHESIANS 4:23–24: "and that you be renewed in the spirit of your mind, and *put on the new self, which in the likeness of God* has been created in righteousness and holiness of the truth."

COLOSSIANS 3:10–11: "and have put on the new self who is being renewed to a true knowledge according to *the image of the One who created him*—a renewal in which there is no distinction between Greek and Jew, circumcised and uncircumcised, barbarian, Scythian, slave and freeman, but Christ is all, and in all."

1 TIMOTHY 4–5: "For *everything created by God is good*, and nothing is to be rejected if it is received with gratitude; for it is sanctified by means of the word of God and prayer."

HEBREWS 1:1–3: "GOD, after He spoke long ago to the fathers in the prophets in many portions and in many ways, in these last days has spoken to us in His Son, whom He appointed heir of all things, through whom also He made the world. And He is the radiance of His glory and the exact representation of His nature, and *upholds all things by the word of His power.*"

HEBREWS 11:3: "*By faith we understand that the worlds were prepared by the word of God, so that what is seen was not made out of things which are visible.*"

JAMES 3:9: "With [the tongue] we bless our Lord and Father, and with it we curse *men, who have been made in the likeness of God;*"

2 PETER 3:3–7: "Know this first of all, that in the last days mockers will come with their mocking, following after their own lusts, and saying, 'Where is the promise of His coming? For ever since the fathers fell asleep, *all continues just as it was from the beginning of creation.*' For when they maintain this, it escapes their notice that *by the word of God the heavens existed* long ago and the earth was formed out of water and by water, through which *the world at that time was destroyed, being flooded with water.* But by His word the present heavens and earth are being reserved for fire, kept for the Day of Judgment and destruction of ungodly men."

REVELATION 4:11: "Worthy are You, our Lord and our God, to receive glory and honor and power; *for You created all things, and because of Your will they existed, and were created.*"

C. S. Lewis addresses the "is the Old Testament in general and the creation story in particular trustworthy?" question this way in *Mere Christianity:*

> I am trying here to prevent anyone saying the really foolish thing that people often say about Him: "I'm ready to accept Jesus as a great moral teacher, but I don't accept His claim to be God." That is the one thing we must not say. A man who said the sort of things Jesus said would not be a great moral teacher. He would either be a lunatic—on a level with the man who says he is a poached egg—or else he would be the Devil of Hell. You must make your choice. Either this man was, and is, the Son of God: or else a madman or something worse. You can shut Him up for a fool, you can spit at Him and kill Him as a demon; or you can fall at His feet and call Him Lord and God. But let us not come with any patronizing nonsense about His being a great human teacher. He has not left that open to us. He did not intend to.

In his first letter to Timothy, whom he had left in charge of the Ephesian church and chose to be his personal representative, Paul references Genesis to substantiate his advice regarding the role of women: "A woman must quietly receive instruction with entire submissiveness. I do not allow a woman to teach or exercise authority over a man, but to remain quiet. For it was Adam who was first created, and then Eve. And it was not Adam who was deceived, but the woman being deceived, fell into transgression" (1 Tim. 2:12–15).

Regardless of whether this passage is considered dated or sexist by modern standards, what is clear is that Paul believed the Genesis account and thought it important enough to base church policy on. He advised Timothy to follow his example.

Added to this, in 2 Corinthians 11:3, Paul says, "But I am afraid that, as the serpent deceived Eve by his craftiness, your minds will be led astray from the simplicity and purity of devotion to Christ." Paul believed in a talking serpent that interacted with Eve, and he joined Jesus in considering Genesis trustworthy. If Paul is misguided in this, how can he be trusted in anything he writes? And so it is with the rest of the New Testament authors. Above all, Christianity is a matter of faith. The more we allow our faith to be diluted by accommodating unbiblical ideas and influences, the faster we move ourselves out of the Christian arena and into a box that includes neither God nor our Savior.

Appendix B

The Spiritual Generations of Israel

Generation	Born (or came of age)	Died	Reference
First	The Land	Egypt	Genesis
Second	Egypt	Egypt	Exodus
Third	Egypt	Desert	Exodus, Leviticus, Numbers
Fourth	Desert	The Land	Deuteronomy and Joshua
Fifth	The Land	The Land	Kings, Former Prophets
Sixth	The Land	Babylon	Latter Prophets
Seventh	Babylon	The Land	Daniel, Ezra, Nehemiah, Chronicles
Eighth	The Land	In Anticipation	Inter-testament Period
Nineth	In Anticipation	Hope in Christ	Gospels, Acts (Eph. 1:12)
Tenth	In Christ	In Christ	Letters, Revelation

Appendix C

Genealogy as Sermon

Genesis 5		
Verse	Name	Meaning
1	Adam	Man
6	Seth	Appointed or Put
9	Enosh	Incurable
12	Kenan	Position
15	Mahalalel	Praise be to God
18	Jared	There is one who will plead for us
21	Enoch	Initiation
25	Methuselah	There shall come
28	Lamech	Powerful overthrower
29	Noah	Rest

Taking the above meanings of the first ten men's names (italicized below) and putting them into a sentence, we have the Gospel:

> *Man* was *put* in an *incurable position*, but *praise be to God, there is one who will plead for us* and by initiation there shall come a *powerful overthrower* who will give us *rest*.

Appendix D

Genesis Cycles

cycle		Genesis Cycles		
	NO HOPE	. . . BUT GOD	WORD or ACT OF LOVE	BUILDING FAITH
1	1:2 – Earth formless and void	1:3 – said, "Let there be light."	2:23 – ". . . this is bone of my bone."	2:24 – Marriage covenant: "Man shall leave his father . . ."
2	3:6 – When the woman saw . . . she ate	3:17 – Cursed the ground	3:21 – God made garments	3:22 – Man like us: knows good and evil
3	4:3 – Cain kills Abel	4:11 – "you are cursed from the ground."	4:25 – Seth appointed	5 – Adam to Noah genealogy
4	6:5 – Wickedness of man great	6:13 – said to Noah . . . gather two . . . of the ground	8:22 – Seedtime and harvest, cold and heat, summer and winter, day and night	9:9 – Noahic covenant with sign of rainbow 8:21 – "I will never curse the ground again."
5	11:1 – Men scattered; language confused	12:1 – called Abram	12:3 – "I will bless those that bless you . . . and in you all the families of the earth will be blessed."	12:7 – Promise: I will give this land to your seed.

cycle		Genesis Cycles		
	NO HOPE	. . . BUT GOD	WORD or ACT OF LOVE	BUILDING FAITH
6	12:10 – Famine in Egypt	12:17 – Plagues on Pharaoh	13:9 – Abram and Lot separate: "the whole land is before me."	13:14 – All the land you see I will give it to you and your descendants forever.
7	14:1 – Lot captive	14:14 – Abram rescues with 318 men	14:17 Blessing of Melchizedek	14:22 I have sworn to take [nothing] lest you say "I have made Abram rich"; 15:1 – "I am a shield to you . . . your reward shall be great"
8	15:2 – Abram has no heir	15:4 – Promise of heir	15:7 – "I am the LORD who brought you out of Ur"	15:18 – Promise: "to your descendants I have given this land"
9	16:1 – Hagar despises Sarai	16:7 – Sends Hagar back	16:11 – Ishmael named by God	16:13 – "I have seen the LORD and lived"
10	17:1 – Abram blamed	17:2 – Changes covenant	17:5 and 15 – Changes names to Abraham and Sarah	17:10 – Abrahamic covenant with sign of circumcision
11	18:3 – Please do not pass me by	18:5 – Turns aside to talk with Abram	18:9 – Promise of Isaac given to Sarah	18:14 – "Is anything too difficult for the LORD?"
12	18:20 – Sodom and Gomorrah	18:17 – Tells Abraham his plan	18:1 – Abraham to command family and do justice, with a promise	18:23 – Abraham intercedes for the righteous of Adamah
13	20:2 – Abimelech takes Sarah	20:6 and 20 – Plagues on Abimelech	20:3–6 – "I did not let you touch her"	20:17 – Abraham prays for Abimelech

cycle		Genesis Cycles		
	NO HOPE	. . . BUT GOD	WORD or ACT OF LOVE	BUILDING FAITH
14	21:10 – Drive out your son	21:12 – Comforts Abraham	21:17 – Call to Hagar from heaven	21:18 – Promise: Ishmael a great nation
15	21:25 – Wells seized	21:22 – "God is with you in all you do"	21:28 – Seven ewes as witness	21:32 – Covenant of Beersheba
16	22:2 – "Offer Isaac"	22:11 – Calls from heaven	22:14 – Jehovah Jireh	22:18 – Promise: "in your seed all nations shall be blessed"
17	23–25 – Isaac's parents die and wife barren	25:21 – Opens Rebekah's womb	25:23 – "two na- tions," "older will serve younger"	26:2 – Covenant extended to Isaac
18	28:1 – Jacob fears Esau	28:12 – Jacob's ladder	28:15 – "I am with you . . . will bring you back"	28:20 – Jacob's vow: The LORD will be my God
19	29–30 – Jacob fears Laban	31:13 – "arise ... and return to the land of your birth"	32:28 – Jacob renamed Israel	32:31 – Jacob limps across Penuel
20	33–34 – Jacob fears Canaanites	35:1 – Terror on cities	35:9 – repeats Israel; v.11 – El Shaddai	35:12 – Covenant extended to Jacob
21	37 – Joseph sold into slavery	39:2 – Was with Joseph	48:3–5 – Jacob adopts Ephraim and Manasseh	48:15–22 – Proph- ecy: Jacob blesses Joseph

Appendix E

Creation Order as a Pattern

Light (Kingdom)	Eden	Abram	Israel	Jesus	The light shines in the darkness
Water Separation Vertical	Fall	Egypt	Egypt	Takes form of man	In the world . . . did not know Him
Water Separation Horizontal	Cain and Able	Lot	Slavery	Tempted	Came to His own, did not receive Him
Plants with seeds	Genesis 5 Genealogy	Promise of seed	Multiplied	Disciples	Word became flesh and dwelt among us
Sun, stars (signs)	Rainbow	Circumcision	Passover	Cross	Star
Fish and birds	From ark	Moriah	Exodus	Resurrection	Dove; fisher of men; Lamb of God
Land animals and man (blessing)	Noah (with blessing) Family	Tribe	Nation	Nations	Firstborn among men

READING DOWN THE COLUMNS, starting with the left-most, the order of creation is listed by days starting with "let there be light" and progressing to the formation of Adam, Hebrew for man. The "light" is not the sunlight we have now—that came on day four. It was the light of the kingdom of God.

Taking Adam forward to Eden where Eve was added, we can progress down column two through the same spiritual steps demonstrated in creation: a separation between God and man (vertical), then between man and man (fratricide), then a listing of descendants (seed), the rainbow as a sign, the post flood exodus from the ark repopulating the earth starting with the release of birds, and ending with a family of eight to repopulate the earth.

The family becomes a tribe in column three, then a nation, then nations, then the world in columns four, five, and six.

Reading across the rows we see the repetition of the creation events. Some are easily seen (rainbow and circumcision as signs); others take reflection (Moriah equivalent to leaving the ark).

The point is that God has always had a plan and a purpose. Using a chart helps us focus on a pattern and understand individual events in the framework of the whole.

Appendix F

Romans

The Cliff Notes for the Pentateuch

THE FIVE BOOKS OF the Pentateuch present a contrast. The contrast is not between Abraham and Moses, but between faith demonstrated by Abraham and the law given by Moses. The "law of Moses" is sometimes called the "law of the Lord"[1] or the "law of righteousness"[2] and is used to distinguish which law, as there are others with various names.

VERSE	LAW OF:
Rom. 3:27	Faith
Rom.7:23	Mind
Rom. 3:27	Sin
Rom. 8:2	Spirit
1 Cor. 9:21	Christ
James 1:25	Liberty

The Pentateuch starts with the big Who I Am of creation, takes a downturn through various falls and sin, and is followed by eleven chapters about Abraham and faith. The rest of Genesis gets Israel into Egypt, and the next four books get them out. Not crossing the border out, but *out-of-Egypt* out. The law was given during this transition as a guide for Israel at the time of the exodus and for everyone else who would be on a spiritual

1. Luke 2:24 and 39.
2. Rom. 9:31.

journey coming out of their own Egypt and bondage. The law is a map for the confused of heart—for anyone whose mind says "go out," but whose heart says "go back." The law is directed at the heart.

In the New Testament there are two major summaries of the Pentateuch. The first is Romans. It starts with a Who I Am: "Paul, a bondservant of Christ Jesus, an apostle, set apart for the gospel of God . . . we have received grace and apostleship to bring about the obedience of faith among the Gentiles."[3] Then there is a downer, chapter one: the Gentiles have had a bad go of things; chapter two, so have the Jews; chapter three, in fact "There is none righteous, not even one,"[4] and worse, "All have sinned and fallen short of the glory of God."[5]

Then there is chapter four—Abraham and faith. Abraham is mentioned twenty-eight times in three chapters of Romans. He is presented as the founder of the Jewish nation,[6] father of the uncircumcised *with faith*,[7] father of the circumcised *with faith*,[8] and father of many nations.[9]

Most of the rest of Romans discusses the law, as was seen in the Pentateuch. As in the Pentateuch the contrast is between faith and works (of the law). As in the Pentateuch there is an eleven-to-one ratio of space given to the law as opposed to faith.[10] Romans is a commentary on the Pentateuch, faith, and the law.

The Pentateuch	Romans
God the Creator	Paul the Apostle
falls	errors
Abraham/Faith	Abraham/Faith
the law	the law

Israel took the law as a model, ignoring Abraham. They particularly ignored Abraham's relationship with Jehovah. The result was law without

3. Rom. 1:1 and 5.

4. Rom. 3:10.

5. Rom. 3:23.

6. Rom. 4:1.

7. Rom. 4:11.

8. Rom. 4:12.

9. Rom. 4:18.

10. Pentateuch: Eleven chapters on faith compared to 118 on law (Exod. 20 on) equals 9.3 percent; Romans: one chapter on faith compared to eleven chapters on law equals 9.1 percent.

faith, and without a relationship with the God of the law. Keeping the law is easier than maintaining relationships. After all, I can interpret the law; I can do it my way. Relationships require the assent of both parties, even if the two parties in relationship are unequal. A relationship with God must be done God's way—he requires faith and belief. You can accept that or reject it, but you can not change it.

The Israelites developed their relationship with the law. They were identified by the law; they justified themselves by the law. Historically they didn't do badly with that tack. Certainly they did better than the Egyptians with their god Ra or the Babylonians with Marduk—Israel is still around. (This is because of a promise Jehovah made to Abraham which is still in force in spite of Israel rather than due to any action on their part.) With the glory days of David and Solomon being ancient history and not even a temple left, there can be little doubt that putting all their eggs in the law basket didn't work.

As easy as it is to criticize the Jews for relying on the works of the law without faith, consideration must be given to the modern church's equally prevalent error: grace without faith. Cheap grace, Martin Luther and Dietrich Bonhoeffer called it. Greasy grace that advertises an easy slide into heaven. Grace with no personal relationship with God.

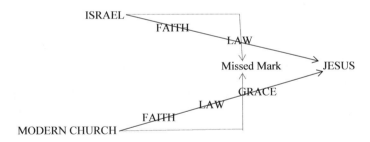

Neither the law without faith nor grace without faith justifies us before God: "For by grace you have been saved through faith; and that not of yourselves, it is the gift of God; not as a result of works, so that no one may boast."[11] But with faith as the basis for a relationship with God and God's Christ, all things are possible. Paul distilled the Pentateuch into a letter to the Romans. His presentation is so powerful that the plan of salvation is easily presented using just a few verses from the epistle—as few as

11. Eph. 2:8–9.

three, but there are so many "and look at this" verses in Paul's letter that the "Romans Road to Salvation" can be as varied as the presenters make it.

Like the law, the Romans Road is a method to help us understand Christ and his salvation. There are other ways—maybe better for any given circumstance or individual— to present the Gospel. But the essence of God's heart is in the Pentateuch and in Romans, given for us to use in our own lives and to impact the lives of others. The Pentateuch is the Gospel analogy, and Romans is the Gospel truth.

When presenting the Romans Road to Salvation, almost everyone cites these verses:

1. ROMANS 3:23: "For all have sinned, and come short of the glory of God."

2. ROMANS 6:23: "For the wages of sin is death; but the gift of God is eternal life through Jesus Christ our Lord."

3. ROMANS 5:8: "But God demonstrates His own love toward us, in that while we were still sinners, Christ died for us."

Most people add,

4. ROMANS 10:9: "that if you confess with your mouth Jesus as Lord, and believe in your heart that God raised Him from the dead, you will be saved" and with it, Romans 10:13: "for everyone who calls on the name of the Lord will be saved."

Also used:

5. ROMANS 5:1: "Therefore, since we have been justified through faith, we have peace with God through our Lord Jesus Christ."

6. ROMANS 8:1 teaches us, "Therefore, there is now no condemnation for those who are in Christ Jesus."

7. ROMANS 3:10: "as it is written, 'There is none righteous, not even one'"

8. ROMANS 1:20: "For since the creation of the world His invisible attributes, His eternal power and divine nature, have been clearly seen, being understood through what has been made, so that they are without excuse."

Two examples from history demonstrate the tragic repercussions that follow failed attempts to evangelize nations eager for the Gospel. In 1286 Pope Nicholas IV received a letter of request from China. The great Chinese emperor Kúblaí Khan, who was well disposed toward Christianity, asked for missionaries to be sent to China. The whole country was open to evangelism. Two friars responded: John of Monte Corvino, a Franciscan, and Dominican Nicholas of Pistoia. Nicholas died on the journey. John built a few churches and was replaced at his death by a few Franciscans, but mostly an opportunity was lost.[12]

Following World War II, General Douglas MacArthur wrote to the president of an American Bible society requesting Bibles and missionaries. The Japanese, defeated in battle, were willing to accept the God of their conquerors as they would have imposed their gods on nations had they won. Few Bibles and fewer missionaries were available, and another opportunity to evangelize a nation was lost.[13]

Both countries are still resistant to the Gospel.

It is unlikely that you will have the door to a nation opened before you, but it is very likely that a door down the street or at work will open. It is absolutely true that the door is open to your children.

Being able to share the Gospel whenever the opportunity is available is a duty all Christians share. The Romans Road can help.

12. The Catholic Encyclopedia online.

13. Personal communication, Bill Gothard.

Appendix G

Hebrews 11

The Official Summary Of The Pentateuch (A Model for Testimonials)

THE SECOND SUMMARY OF the Pentateuch in the New Testament is a single chapter in Hebrews: the Hall of Faith.

Faith starts simply: believe God is. Then add to belief: seek Him. These two steps of faith are illustrated in Hebrews 11, first by the major test of faith—do you believe God created you?—and then by Abel and Enoch, who sought after God when others wouldn't. To avoid a formula, the Bible does not tell us exactly what they did, but it is always about where your heart is. So begins a walk of faith. Everyone walking with God has a story, a testimony. While they seem different, and in fact they will be different, most conversion accounts follow a common pattern.

Although every Christian has a testimony, some are not ready to share. However, it is wise to consider that a personal testimony, thoughtfully prepared and sincerely shared, can make the difference between heaven and hell for someone in your future. It is a story and as such can have all the power and persuasion of the great stories of the Bible, *if* it is told effectively.

Almost all testimonies have the same general format, with blanks to fill in. First is a "who I was" segment. That segment falls into one of four categories based on what you perceived your relationship was to religion and whether you were struggling financially.

Then . . . something happened and the story is on. It looks like this:

			AT THE TIME	
when I realized there was something missing			$ $ $	
			+	**-**
P A S T	C H U R C H	**+**	Paul	Peter
		-	Matthew	Thief on the cross

It doesn't matter which box you started in—everyone starts lost in spiritual Egypt. Some starts have more robust histories: Paul has a lot to say about who he was before the Damascus Road encounter; other starts are more bust: the thief on the cross with Jesus probably did not have much to tell (although owning a sordid past highlights the redemptive power of Christ and can be the start of a compelling testimony).

1. Something was missing, it was Jesus.

2. I started: church, Bible study, talking with someone.

3. I accepted Christ as Savior.

4. I was baptized.

5. Then I began to understand the Holy Spirit and the promises of God. I started to see the things of God working in my life.

6. Next came changes in my life—friends, habits, hang-ups.

7. My priorities changed: time (more prayer or learning), money (tithe), goals (how I see myself).

8. I wanted to be a part of what God in doing.

9. I can say that I have been grafted into the Tree of Life—the Christian family.

10. God has been faithful.

If you haven't polished up your own testimony, you might find it helpful to write down personalized responses to these points, then pray for the Lord to lead you to someone you can share your story with. This is not a bad pattern. It comes right out of Hebrews 11.

TESTIMONY	HEB. 11	STEP OF FAITH
Missing something	3	Believe God is
Started	4–6	Seek God
Accepted Christ	7	Reverence
Baptized	8	Obedience
Things of God	11	Receive
Changes	13 and 16	Be separate
Priorities	17	Offer up all
What God is doing	20	Spiritual vision
Grafted in	21	Sonship
Faithful	22	Faithfulness

Relating to the people that Hebrews 11 associates with these steps can sharpen our understanding and witness.

1. Believe God is. Foundational to all civilizations is a belief in some god. The key is that you believe Jesus is God.

2. Seek God. All we know about Enoch is that he walked with God, God took him, and he didn't see death. Faith increases as we broaden our search for God. Seek and keep seeking. Think for a minute of Jesus on Golgotha, and consider who was watching: some of his followers, some Pharisees, and, because crucifixions took place beside highways where they could be seen, some travelers and the curious. Even the Pharisees, who took a stand but were wrong, were given more credit by Jesus than those who weren't paying attention.

HOT	COLD	LUKEWARM
Disciples	Pharisees	Travelers
I love	I hate	I don't care

3. Revere God. Noah took a lot of abuse while he was building the ark. One hundred years of ridicule. He feared God more than man.

4. Obey God. Abraham obeyed by going to a place he did not know. Sometimes we go when called, sometimes we aren't called, or are we are called to go somewhere else (think Jonah). If God isn't blessing you where you are, remember, *going* was the obedience for Abraham, not being there.

5. Receive from God. Sarah at age ninety received the ability to conceive. God uses all willing vessels and without limitation.

6. Be separate. All of the above individuals considered themselves exiles on the earth. They *did not* desire to go back to their old ways as Israel did in the exodus.

7. Offer up all. Abraham laid Isaac on the alter and raised the knife to sacrifice him to Jehovah, considering that He was able to do anything—even raise Isaac from the dead. He didn't withhold Isaac from God or God from Isaac.

8. Gain spiritual vision. Isaac himself, after hearing the voice of Jehovah Jireh on Mt. Moriah and sacrificing the ram He provided, blessed his own sons based on God's plan of salvation.

9. Treasure your status as a son or daughter. Jacob, having received his father's vision, adopted Joseph's sons as his own, rescuing them from Egypt and joining them to Israel. He was leaning on his staff (v. 21), the result of his wrestling with God and man to obtain the birthright, the inheritance, and the blessing of Jehovah. These were the most important things in his life, treasures he gave to Manasseh and Ephraim.

10. Remain faithful: Joseph, the second most powerful man on earth in his time, also disclaimed Egypt. He did it while he was in power and rich, and hundreds of years in advance, declaring his belief in Jehovah and claiming his place among Israel.

There is a pattern of cycles in the presentation of the Pentateuch (see Appendix D). There is a pattern in the creation that is repeated on through the Pentateuch and the Gospel of John (see Appendix E). There is a pattern presented in the Hebrews 11 summary which is also in Romans (see Appendix H).

The pattern is one of growing in faith, and growing in faith is your testimony. It starts with a simple but large step—believe God is who He says. It proceeds by increments to full reliance on God's grace and a life *in* the world but not *of* the world.

Appendix H

Genesis Summarized and Condensed

Step of Faith	Hebrews 11 Verse(s)	Romans Verse(s)
Believe God is	3: worlds were prepared by the Word of God. 6: he who comes to God must believe that He is	1:18–20 "since the creation . . . His eternal power and divine nature . . . have been clearly perceived. . . through what has been made"
Seek God	4: Abel offered to God a better sacrifice 6: [God] is a rewarder of those who seek Him.	1:21–23: "though they knew God, they did not honor Him . . . and exchanged the glory of the incorruptible God for an image"
Revere God	7: Noah . . . in reverence prepared an ark for the salvation of his household	1:25: "they exchanged the truth of God for the lie, and worshiped and served the creature rather than the Creator"
Obey God	8: Abraham, when he was called, obeyed	4:21: "[Abraham] being fully assured that what God had promised, He was able also to perform"
Receive from God	11: Sarah herself received ability (literally power) to conceive	5:15–16: "the gracious gift is not like the offense . . . [it] arose from many transgressions resulting in justification."

Be separate	13–16: All these died in faith . . . having confessed that they were strangers and exiles on the earth . . . desire a better country, a heavenly one	6:4: "we have been buried with Him through baptism into death, so that just as Christ was raised from the dead through the glory of the Father, so we too might walk in newness of life."
Offer up all	17: Abraham, when he was tested, offered up Isaac, his only son	6:18: "having been freed from sin, you became slaves of righteousness"
Gain vision	20: Isaac blessed Jacob and Esau, even regarding things to come	8:5: "For those who are in accord with the flesh set their minds on the things of the flesh, but those who are in accord with the Spirit, the things of the Spirit."
Treasure sonship	21: Jacob, as he was dying, blessed each of the sons of Joseph	8:14: "For all who are being led by the Spirit of God, these are sons and daughters of God." 9:8: ". . . it is not the children of the flesh who are children of God, but the children of the promise are regarded as descendants."
Remain faithful	22: Joseph, when he was dying, gave orders concerning his bones.	12:2: . . . do not be conformed to this world, but be transformed by the renewing of your mind, so that you may prove what the will of God is, that which is good and acceptable and perfect.

Appendix I

The Gospel Viewed in the Constellations

PSALM 19:1–4 (NIV) IS a beautiful testament of God's heavenly message:

> The heavens declare the glory of God;
>   the skies proclaim the work of his hands.
> Day after day they pour forth speech;
>   night after night they reveal knowledge.
> They have no speech, they use no words;
>   no sound is heard from them.
> Yet their voice goes out into all the earth,
>   their words to the ends of the world.

In Genesis 15, Abram asks God, what good is the reward that God promised since I am childless, "and the heir of my house is Eliezer of Damascus? . . . Since You have given me no son . . ." In answer, the LORD takes him outside and tells Abram to "count" the stars.

We discussed this exchange in cycle 8, but here is what Barry Setterfield says about it on his Gospel in the Stars website:

> In the Hebrew, the word which becomes "count" in English is "caphar," which means "to score, to mark as a tally, to record, to inscribe, to recount, to celebrate or enumerate. Also to talk or to tell out." It comes from a root meaning "a book" or "a scroll." . . . The word in the Greek is "arithmos" which is "something as reckoned up," coming from "airo," meaning "to lift, to take up, to take away." The meaning of "arithmos," is much wider than "count" and can mean "enumerate" or "reckon." In the LXX, the word translated

"number," from "if you can number them," has the prefix, "ek" or "ex" [which] means "among, because of, between, from, by means of, etc." The word itself then is ekarithmos (or exarithmos).

God did not tell Abraham to count the stars. That is not the translation of the word used in the Hebrew. God told him to "recount" or "tell" the stars. There was a story there that God wanted Abraham to take note of. And there was something about this story that Abraham believed and it was counted to him as righteousness.[1]

The ecliptic is the apparent path of the sun across the sky. Due to seasonal changes, it varies nine degrees on each side of the mean, making a band. In the night sky, constellations that are visible in that band as a group are called the zodiac. The planets and our moon are in the same plane and are variably superimposed on the constellations in varying fashion as they circle the sun in markedly different time frames.

Add shooting stars, novas, and comets to the changing alignments, and you're adding opportunity for soothsayers, magicians, and charlatans to predict the future, near and far. Astrology started early in star observation history, and words like zodiac, which means circle of animals (even though not all of the constellations are animals),[2] have been so strongly associated with fortune-telling as to be made useless for anything else.

However, as Setterfield notes:

> The specific twelve constellations we recognize today as the zodiac is [sic] referred to as the Mazzaroth in Hebrew. We find this word used in Job 38:32, which means the word was in use extraordinarily early, as Job is probably the earliest completed book of the Bible, written about 2900 BC. In Job 26:13, Job says God formed the constellation figures. In Job 38:31–32, the Pleiades and Orion are both mentioned by name.[3]

The ecliptic has from early times been allocated into twelve equal divisions of thirty degrees each, called "signs." The constellations loosely associated with the divisions or signs, however, due to the wobble of the earth's axis known as precession, have long been known to be changing. It

1. https://barrysetterfield.org/stargospel.html. This is one of several very good websites devoted to this topic. They have much more depth than we can get into here.

2. barrysetterfield.org. The word itself comes from "zoad," the Greek word for a way, a path, a step, or circuit. (Every planet or revolving body has its own "zodiac,"— the "zodiac of Mars" for instance.

3. With some rearranging by me.

takes 26,000 years for a complete rotation of the zodiac, or a change of one constellation every two thousand years, give or take as the constellations are of varying widths.

Ptolemy (AD 100–170) was famous as both an astronomer and astrologer. He "clearly explained the theoretical basis of the western zodiac as being a tropical coordinate system, by which the zodiac is aligned to the equinoxes and solstices, rather than the visible constellations that bear the same names as the zodiac signs."[4]

Many authors have associated the zodiac with Bible passages. E. W. Bullinger interpreted the creatures appearing in the books of Ezekiel and Revelation as the middle signs of the four quarters of the zodiac, with the lion as Leo, the bull as Taurus, the man representing Aquarius, and the eagle representing Scorpio.[5]

In spite of the unfortunate, inextricable linking of the zodiac and astrology, and precession notwithstanding, the order of the constellation in the ecliptic does not change. What Abraham saw, we see today. So our question should be not "How many stars did Abraham see?" but "What story did God show Abraham in the stars?"

The story was a life changer. "No heir" went from his first known complaint to Jehovah to never being mentioned again, even though he had other questions ("How will I know I will possess the land?"), and even when he was told to take Isaac to Mt. Moriah.

If the circle of constellations is a story, where does it start? Due to the precession of the equinoxes, the constellation on the horizon at the rising of the sun on the spring equinox (or any other specified time) has changed over time. How much time is anyone's guess—there is no shortage of evangelists for one theory or another. Abraham had an advantage—he started where God told him to start.

If we begin with Jesus' birth, we start at Virgo, the virgin and end with Leo, the lion. Barry Setterfield has a list of the constellations and their meanings on his website (cited above), and there are several books that have details of the constellations, sub-constellations, and Alpha stars whose names' meanings add to the account. What emerges is not a story with an order from start to finish so much ac vignettes that together form a message.

4. http://en.wikipedia.org/wiki/Zodiac.

5. Gopakumar. *The Great Year and Virgin Comets*, 34.

Bibliography

Amaral, Joe. *Story in the Stars: Discovering God's Design and Plan for Our Universe*. New York: Hachette, 2018.

Chambers, Oswald. *My Utmost for His Highest*. Grand Rapids, MI: Discovery House, 2010.

Chrysostom, St. John. *Homilies of Genesis 18-45 Homily 32*. Fathers of the Church 75. Washington, DC: Catholic University of America Press, 1990.

Fohrman, David. *Genesis: A Parsha Companion*. Jerusalem: Maggid, 2020.

Gilder, George. *Telecosm*. New York: Free, 2002.

Gopakumar, K. G. *The Great Year and Virgin Comets*. https://www.obooko.com/free-new-age-astrology-occult-books/great-year-virgin-comets.

Hebrewversity. "hebrew-origins-adams-name-connection-ground." https://www.hebrewversity.com.

Kass, Leon R. *The Beginning of Wisdom: Reading Genesis*. New York: Free, 2003.

Pangle, Thomas L. *Political Philosophy and the God of Abraham*. Baltimore, MD: Johns Hopkins University Press, 2003.

Sailhammer, John H. *The Pentateuch as Narrative: a Biblical-Theological Commentary*. Grand Rapids, MI: Zondervan, 1992.

Sefaria. https://www.sefaria.org/Rashi_on_Genesis.

Setterfield, Barry. https://barrysetterfield.org/stargospel.html.

Strong, James. *The Exhaustive Concordance of the Bible*. Nashville, TN: Abingdon, 1975.

Whiston, William. *The Works of Josephus*. Peabody, MA: Hendrickson, 2001.